"Take a thought provoking topic, mix it with Jay Payleitner's witty, conversational writing style and irrefutable knowledge of Scripture, and what do you get? An entertaining and inspiring reading experience that will inform and challenge even well-read believers. *If God Were Your Life Coach* is another must read from Jay."

Ken Blanchard, coauthor of
The New One Minute Manager and *Lead Like Jesus*

"Reading Jay's book is like sitting in a real office with a real appointment with the real Jesus. Profound! The just-right readings are spot on!"

Jon Gauger, radio host, Moody Radio Network
and author of *If I Could Do It All Over Again*

"Great coaches ask great questions! In Jay Payleitner's new book, *If God Were Your Life Coach,* you will experience God asking you great questions like, 'What do you want me to do for you?'"

Bob Tiede, CRU leadership development team
and author of *Great Leaders Ask Questions*

"Jay has tapped into something much greater than just the counsel of a life coach. He's invited readers to an encounter with the designer and sustainer of life itself . . . someone whose purpose and deepest desire is to make our journey through this life mind-blowingly abundant and complete."

Tom Dewey, Director of Operations,
Transforming Center

"Encouraging. Honest. Practical. A creative approach to biblical self-examination that felt like a welcomed coaching session. This book will help you evaluate your goals, habits, and motivations in light of God's calling for your life."

Todd Cartmell, Psy.D., child psychologist
and author of *8 Simple Tools for Raising Great Kids*

"Brilliant! *If God Were Your Life Coach* is a well thought out devotional that will bless anyone seeking clear direction for their life. These are great questions that God IS asking us in Scripture."

Tom Cheshire, founder,
Relevant Practical Ministry for Men

"Jay's book raises critical questions and relights my Christian fire to find meaning and purpose in my life."

Michael Penny, President, Strategy Conversions, Inc.
and adjunct professor at Judson University

"In *If God Were Your Life Coach*, Jay Payleitner combines the truth of Scripture with relatable insights. These succinct conversations with the ultimate life coach will help you gain wisdom."

Matt Guevara, Executive Director,
International Network of Children's Ministry

"Here's your chance to imagine if God were your life coach. Don't be surprised if Scripture begins to press upon your heart in a new way and lead you to live the story line that God desires of you."

Rev. Dr. John Nelson, Pastor

IF
God
WERE YOUR
Life
Coach

60 WORDS OF WISDOM
FROM THE ONE WHO KNOWS YOU BEST

JAY PAYLEITNER

WORTHY®
Inspired

Published by Worthy Inspired, an imprint of Worthy Publishing Group, a division of Worthy Media, Inc., One Franklin Park, 6100 Tower Circle, Suite 210, Franklin, TN 37067.

WORTHY is a registered trademark of Worthy Media, Inc.

HELPING PEOPLE EXPERIENCE THE HEART OF GOD

Library of Congress Cataloging-in-Publication Data

Names: Payleitner, Jay K., author.
Title: If God were your life coach : 60 words of wisdom from the one who
    knows you best / by Jay Payleitner.
Description: Franklin, TN : Worthy Publishing, 2017.
Identifiers: LCCN 2017000687 | ISBN 9781617958564 (tradepaper)
Subjects: LCSH: Success--Religious aspects--Christianity--Miscellanea. |
    Success--Biblical teaching--Miscellanea. | Christian life--Biblical
    teaching--Miscellanea.
Classification: LCC BV4598.3 .P39 2017 | DDC 248.4--dc23
LC record available at https://lccn.loc.gov/2017000687

For foreign and subsidiary rights, contact rights@worthypublishing.com

ISBN: 978-1-61795-856-4

Cover Design: MTWdesign.net
Cover Photo: Shutterstock.com

Printed in the United States of America
17 18 19 20 21 LSC 10 9 8 7 6 5 4 3 2

To Rita Anne.
Sharing life radiantly since 1979.

Imagine

Imagine the Creator of the Universe sitting across from you as you map out your day, week, and life. He knows you're at a crossroads. He knows there are several paths you can take.

He also knows your gifts and talents. After all, they came directly from his generous hand. He knows your hopes and dreams. And even has a few wonderful surprises waiting just for you. He sees every obstacle and hurdle that lies ahead. Some he placed there to sharpen you and prepare you for future challenges.

Now imagine his voice. As your new life coach, each spoken word is a gift chosen just for you. Perhaps a question to make you think. A warning to help you prepare. A clear truth to give you confidence. All words of love.

On the first page of each chapter, you'll find the imagined voice of God along with the Bible verse that inspired it. Before turning to the next page, you're invited to pause and really contemplate the voice and the verse.

Then, the final two or three pages of each chapter will help you unpack and dig deeper into that question, warning, or truth.

The sixty chapters are short. Easy to read. And nothing in these pages will make you feel like damaged goods. Just the opposite. Each session will leave you with the thought, *I can do this.*

Wherever you are in life, God is already preparing you for the next big thing. You're just about ready and you don't even know it. This book—and time spent with God as your life coach—may be the springboard for a remarkable and unforgettable season of life.

Would it help to picture God and the room in which you meet? Of course, God's actual appearance and the glory of heaven are beyond our imagination. But, if you like, you are quite welcome to visualize a distinguished mentor enthroned in a magnificent leather chair in a study lined with bookshelves. Hardwood floors. Sunbeams flowing through long windows. A voice that's strong, comforting, and reassuring.

More important than the physical nature of God as your life coach is the nature of His truth and love and righteousness. God can be trusted. And He has a message you'll want to hear. Listen.

1

How are **you** today?

Today, if you hear his voice. . . .

HEBREWS 3:7

A casual sincere greeting is exactly what you might expect when you connect with a life coach. "How are you today?" But somehow the question sounds different coming from the Creator of the Universe.

His voice doesn't sound like anything you've ever heard before.

Have you imagined God's voice? At the baptism of Jesus, you certainly imagined a sincere fatherly tone resounding the words, "You are my Son, whom I love; with you I am well pleased" (Mark 1:11). If you're sincere about asking God to be your life coach, that vocal quality would bring you comfort and confidence. And that kind of message is exactly what you would be hoping for.

Throughout Scripture, God's voice seems to take on a variety of tonal qualities. In Acts 9, God's voice would come across as profoundly ominous after a heavenly light thunders across the road to Damascus and Saul is knocked to the ground. "Saul, Saul, why do you persecute me?" The encounter left the murderous zealot blind and ultimately transformed.

Of course, Adam and Eve heard God's voice in the Garden of Eden and were more than a little afraid (Genesis 3:10). Fear of God is a good thing, especially if you've just been hanging out with a crafty and influential serpent. When God called to the man, "Where are you?" you may imagine the voice similar to that of a father preparing to discipline his seven-year-old, who should have known better than to leave his new bicycle in the driveway. There's a reason we call God, "Heavenly Father."

Moses, Abraham, Samuel, and David all heard the audible voice of God. Right out loud. It's actually possible that you may also experience that miraculous blessing. But walk carefully. There are way too many crooks, false preachers, and self-serving hotshots claiming some version of, "God told me. . . ." More times than not, their supposedly audible mandates cannot be supported in the Bible, and there is no group of wise counselors ready to hold those charlatans accountable.

This book returns chapter-by-chapter to Scripture for life-coaching advice. Otherwise, you may as well be reading one of the other ten gazillion books on how to be a success in the eyes of the world. This book makes no such promises.

Still, no matter what you read—here or anywhere— keep listening for God's voice in your life. Whether audible, from a trusted friend, in a reliable publication, or a still, small, barely perceptible whisper. He has only good things to say and he does care about how you are today.

2

No, really. How are you?
Unlike most of the time
you hear that question,
I am actually hoping
for an answer.

People will be lovers of themselves, lovers of money, boastful,
proud, abusive, disobedient to their parents, ungrateful,
unholy, without love, unforgiving, slanderous,
without self-control, brutal, not lovers of the good.

2 TIMOTHY 3:2-5

During the course of a routine day, you may hear some version of that phrase more than a dozen times. "How you doin'?" "Hey, how are you?" "Wassup?" But if you're honest, you'll admit that most of the time the greeter doesn't really mean it. To be even more honest, most of the time you say such things, you don't really mean them either.

That's okay. That's even expected. Don't beat up on yourself.

Most people really are more worried about themselves than others. Especially in the course of a busy day. We have things to do, people to see, million-dollar deals to negotiate. It's not that we're monsters. We politely smile and speak words of greeting, but we don't really have the time or desire to start a real conversation.

If we see a neighbor in their driveway, we imagine the worst-case scenario: We say, "Hi, how are you?" And they reply, "Well I'm mostly fine. But I have this killer toothache, and my health insurance rates just went up again, and my car engine is knocking like a vinyl siding salesman, and my teenage son just got a face tattoo, and my water softener is out of salt, and it would be great if you could carry these forty-pound bags of salt into my basement."

Not many people want to be part of that conversation. Does that mean we are being self-centered? In a word, yes. But that's part of the human condition. Consider the description from the third chapter of 2 Timothy. Continue reading in that chapter and you'll discover those words describe people living in the end times. In other words, the farther we get from Jesus, the more likely we are to be proud, ungrateful, unloving, brutal, and so on.

What does that mean for anyone beginning this journey of God as your life coach? Step one might be to admit your selfishness. Sure, you're not the worst person in town. The guy down the street is meaner and more self-centered than you'll ever be. The woman in your power Pilates class is a total she-devil. But you must admit, most people do generally care more about themselves than the rest of the world. Without a doubt, when it comes to beloved members of your family, you sacrifice greatly and would even give your life. But caring for strangers and acquaintances is not typical human behavior.

We're just being honest here. If this sixty-chapter process is going to work, we need to set that as a ground rule. Commit to honest and open self-appraisals. Don't live in denial. Don't pretend you've got things under control. Admit you have needs. Be a little vulnerable.

Then God—your life coach for this adventure—just might be able to use you in ways you would never expect.

3

You see, I do care.
You are what I care about most.

For the LORD your God is living among you.
He is a mighty savior. He will take delight in you
with gladness. With his love, he will calm all your fears.
He will rejoice over you with joyful songs.

ZEPHANIAH 3:17 NLT

If you're going to allow God to be your life coach, you're going to have to trust him. This Old Testament verse offers you a five-part reason why you can put your life in his hands.

First, he is with you. Some people imagine God as a far-off impersonal being who swoops in once in a while to punish or rescue. That couldn't be further from the truth. He created you. He cares about you. He knows you well. He also knows about the dangers of this fallen world. He's not going to leave you to fend for yourself. Even during difficult moments when he may seem far away, he's holding you in his loving grasp. Isaiah 49:15-16 says, "I will not forget you! See, I have engraved you on the palms of my hands."

Second, he's strong enough to deliver on his promises. He didn't only create you, he created the entire universe. The word "mighty" is an understatement. The word "savior" is undeniable.

Third, this passage from Zephaniah confirms that you are delightful to him. When we think about God we should be awestruck and overwhelmed. When God thinks about us, he is delighted. Feel free to imagine him smiling with pride. Even when we mess up, he looks into our hearts and sees that we are seeking him.

Fourth, with God on our side we need never be afraid. Because we're human, fears will bubble up into our lives, but he promises to calm them. That's the great power of his love. Fear vanishes.

Fifth, our existence makes God sing for joy. Which seems quite remarkable. But actually it makes great sense considering our whole purpose is to give him glory.

So when God says, "How are you?" he really does want to know how you are. He wants to know what's on your mind. Your hopes and dreams. Your frustrations and failures. Go ahead and tell him all the things you might reveal to a human life coach in the first few sessions.

Of course, God already knows. He is God after all. But he also wants you to know that he cares. When he asks questions, he is helping you focus your aspirations and unpack the gifts, tools, and resources already at your disposal.

4

My Child . . .
I'd like to help,
if you'll let me.

---

*Trust in the LORD with all your heart
and lean not on your own understanding.*

PROVERBS 3:5

This much-loved proverb delivers the most essential decision you need to make when you enlist God to be your life coach. Trust not in yourself. Instead lean on God. He can handle the full weight of everything that comes your way. All you have to do is ask. He is all-knowing, all-present, all-powerful.

But the one thing God can't do is make that decision for you. That's on you.

Letting go of our own way of thinking and choosing to trust someone else is never easy. We have our preconceived notions and established patterns. "This is the way I've always done it." "I'm comfortable with the ways things are." "If it's not broken, don't fix it."

That's why we have to be intentional about setting aside our old way of thinking. We're stuck in our own rut of what we know and how we do things. Our heart dreams about new and better ways to experience life. Our head rejects that idea.

How often do we fail to take advice from someone who is in a position to actually show us a better way? We sit in a classroom and think we know more than the teachers. We hire a coach to improve our public speaking skills, tennis backhand, or exercise regime, but as soon as the consultation is over we return to our old bad habits.

It's not that we're afraid of change. It's just that we don't like it. Sticking with the status quo is much easier.

Still, there's something very attractive about the fifteen words of Proverbs 3:5. We want to let go and let God.

Here's an idea. When you come across a compelling bit of Scripture—on a poster, from a speaker, in a book like this—take the mind-expanding step of reading that verse in context. You'd be surprised at how often the words surrounding a passage adds depth, fresh understanding, and clarification to the initial idea. In other words, if you like Proverbs 3:5, read all of Proverbs 3.

Here's just a taste.

Do not forget my teaching, but keep my commands in your heart, for they will prolong your life many years and bring you peace and prosperity. (Proverbs 3:1-2)

In all your ways submit to him, and he will make your paths straight. (Proverbs 3:6)

Do not be wise in your own eyes; fear the Lord and shun evil. (Proverbs 3:7)

Do not let wisdom and understanding out of your sight, preserve sound judgment and discretion; they will be life for you. (Proverbs 3:21-22)

The Lord's curse is on the house of the wicked, but he blesses the home of the righteous. (Proverbs 3:33)

There is a better way. We just don't know it. Yet.

So, are you ready to trust, lean, submit, fear, and be wise?

5

Let's start with
a few questions.

Jesus stopped and ordered the man to be brought to him.
When he came near, Jesus asked him,
"What do you want me to do for you?"
"LORD, I want to see," he replied.

LUKE 18:40-41

15

See if you can relate to the man in this true story from the gospel of Luke. I know he's blind. He's a beggar. And someone you may not instantly relate to. But, if you stop and consider his plight, you will realize both his ailments are common to all humankind.

I confess that if I saw him on a Chicago sidewalk shaking a cup or holding a sign asking for money, most of the time I would walk past with little change of expression. While the image of those less fortunate souls always stays with me, rarely do I stop and help them out. And I certainly don't identify with them.

I'm not blind. Nor have I ever asked for a handout. (Or am I? And have I?)

As Jesus approached Jericho, a blind man was sitting by the roadside begging. When he heard the crowd going by, he asked what was happening. They told him, "Jesus of Nazareth is passing by."

He called out, "Jesus, Son of David, have mercy on me!"

Those who led the way rebuked him and told him to be quiet, but he shouted all the more, "Son of David, have mercy on me!"

Jesus stopped and ordered the man to be brought to him. When he came near, Jesus asked him, "What do you want me to do for you?"

"Lord, I want to see," he replied.

Jesus said to him, "Receive your sight; your faith has healed you." (Luke 18:35-43)

So often, when you open the Bible, you'll find a passage with multiple meanings and applications. This story of Jesus healing the blind beggar could certainly be a reminder to help the less fortunate. It could also be a lesson in how we should approach Jesus with a humble and broken spirit, "Have mercy on me." In the blind beggar, we also find a model of persistence and faith.

Still, there's another lesson that's equally as compelling and applicable to our lives. Tucked in this real life drama is a strategy of how we relate to God as our life coach. We can be sure that Jesus knows what the man needs. Jesus already knows his physical impairment and what's in the man's heart. Still Jesus asks, "What do you want me to do for you?" The man replies with a specific request. And Jesus delivers.

In other words, don't be wishy-washy when your life coach asks questions. Be honest and sincere. Admit your blind and broken condition. It's okay if you don't have all the answers. Discerning your gifts and goals is an ongoing process. Even when you finish chapter 60 and close this book, there will still be many unanswered questions. And that's okay.

Never fear questions. They help get to the heart of what really matters. Expect Jesus to be sincerely and constantly asking, "What do you want me to do for you?"

6

What brought you here?

Draw near to God,
and he will draw near to you.

JAMES 4:8 ESV

Here you are six short chapters into a book in which you're asking God to be your life coach. The question is . . . why? What brought you here?

I suspect it's because you want more out of life. Just like all of us.

As we settle into the adult phase of our time here on earth, we begin to have a gnawing feeling that there's some elusive secret to life—something beyond ourselves—and in typical human fashion we invest a lot of our own time and energy trying to figure it out. So we try things. Good things and not-so-good things. Advanced education. High-powered careers. Sex. Drugs. Alcohol. Political causes. Anti-political causes. Alternative lifestyles. Alternative religions. Military service. Art. Music. Money. Power. Some people don't have any kind of plan; they just figure their life purpose is to rebel against their parents, the government, the establishment, or God himself.

This quest for meaning could be described as an effort to fill a universal human void. I agree with Blaise Pascal, the seventeenth-century mathematician and philosopher, who described the void as an abyss, a God-shaped hole in the heart of every man.

"All men seek happiness. This is without exception. Whatever different means they employ, they all tend to this end...the mark and empty trace, which he in vain tries to fill from all his surroundings, seeking from things absent the help he does not obtain in things present... But these are all inadequate, because the infinite abyss can only be filled by an infinite and immutable Object, that is to say, only by God Himself."

Intentionally or unknowingly, most of us spend our life attempting to fill that infinite abyss. And you know what? That quest is never in vain. The quest is noble! Yes, we may take a wrong path or stumble in our pilgrimage. But if we continue to seek the highest purpose—truth, justice, righteousness, love—we will eventually find the one true God.

God is reaching out to all of us, but it's still up to each of us to reach back. The familiar passage from the gospel of Matthew confirms, "Ask and it will be given to you; seek and you will find; knock and the door will be opened to you" (Matthew 7:7). The Old Testament encourages us to put our whole heart and soul into the pursuit of truth, "You will find him if you seek him with all your heart and with all your soul" (Deuteronomy 4:29).

It's okay to admit that you're pursuing God. Seek his face. Turn to him. And he will turn to you.

7

What do you **want**?

Just for fun, let's play a little game. Let's say you really did have a life coach who could steer you toward a life of satisfaction and fulfillment. Off the top of your head, without too much deliberation, what might be your top seven goals? Would your list look something like this: wealth, rest, fame, power, honor, great sex, and guilt-free feasting?

Sound good? It does to me. The items on your list give you resources and influence to do worthwhile things. Plus you've included a few physical pleasures to make you happier than a seagull with a French fry. I'm pretty sure these seven items would be high up on almost anyone's bucket list. Sure, they're a bit self-focused, but it's your list, right?

Well, let's take another look at that list. Closer scrutiny reveals that it's pretty much a restatement of another list commonly called "The Seven Deadly Sins," only with words that are slightly less abrasive. The seven deadly sins are not specifically listed in Scripture, but they are universally acknowledged as a good place to start when reflecting on the sin in our life. Here they are: greed, sloth, envy, wrath, pride, lust, gluttony.

"Wait a second," you say. "Don't saddle me with those nasty labels."

Sorry, but as an inhabitant of this planet you're already infected with all those weaknesses to some degree or another. The Bible confirms—and you really can't deny—that most human failings are fairly obvious.

The acts of the flesh are obvious: sexual immorality, impurity and debauchery; idolatry and witchcraft; hatred, discord, jealousy, fits of rage, selfish ambition, dissensions, factions and envy; drunkenness, orgies, and the like. I warn you, as I did before, that those who live like this will not inherit the kingdom of God. (Galatians 5:19-21)

I hope you agree those three verses are disturbing to read. But if you consider the character traits one at a time, you may be finding yourself saying, "That's not me. That's not me. That's not me." Then suddenly, "Yikes. I confess there's one or two or three of which I am undeniably guilty."

Without heaping on any more guilt, let's take a step back and suggest that we all need to put a little more thought into answering the question, "What do you want?" The impulsive, knee-jerk answers are more wealth, more sleep, more power, and so on. (Proving once again we're human.) But you're clearly hoping for a life with more significance. If you were dealing with a mere human life coach, you might settle for those things that don't have eternal value. As a matter of fact, helping their clients find temporal happiness is the focus of most professional life coaches.

So let's turn our attention back to the question at the top of this chapter and try again.

8

What do you **really** want?
Because, I have
what you **need**.

But seek first his kingdom and his righteousness,
and all these things will be given to you as well.

MATTHEW 6:33

Now we're talking. Matthew 6:33 puts first things first. We're finally admitting that God's way might be better than our way. By seeking the reality of God, we have the Bible's guarantee that he's going to make sure we have everything we need.

Which brings us to an important distinction: the difference between needs and wants.

Anyone who has been to a supermarket with a three-year-old knows there's a big difference between needs and wants. Little Billy thinks he needs Sugar-O's, licorice whips, and a 25-cent ride on the mechanical horsey, but he's wrong of course. Those are wants.

Similarly, you and I want the latest technology on our desks, in our pockets, and on our wrists. We want dessert. We want a sweet ride. We want to look good and live well. We actually have a pretty long list. When really all we need is food, shelter, clothing . . . and God.

The difference between needs and wants is illustrated almost comically in the second book of the Bible. You know the story. God sends plagues to Egypt enabling the Israelites to escape from Pharaoh's wicked ways. God miraculously parts the Red Sea. When Moses takes a little too long coming down Mt. Sinai with the Ten Commandments, the Israelites cast a golden calf as their idol. God is ready to destroy the entire nation, but Moses begs for mercy.

This is all serious stuff, but early in their forty-year trek across the desert, the people of Israel prove that they don't know the difference between wants and needs. Bored and hungry they whine to Moses, "If only we had died by the Lord's hand in Egypt! There we sat around pots of meat and ate all the food we wanted, but you have brought us out into this desert to starve this entire assembly to death" (Exodus 16:3). After hearing their grumbling, God provides their daily bread every morning in the form of manna. It tastes like wafers made with honey! All they have to do is walk out of their tents every morning and gather it, yet still they complain and fail to follow instructions.

The takeaway from our heavenly life coach is this: choose to follow. Trust your needs will be met. If it doesn't turn out exactly as you hope, be patient. Although it took a while, the Israelites did actually make it to the Promised Land. And in God's timing, so will you.

One final note: There's a very good chance that what God has in store for you is significantly bigger, better, and awesomer than your original vision. That's right. Your want is too small. So seek first God's kingdom and keep your expectations high.

9

Are you ready to **commit**?
I am waiting
to empower you.

---

*For the eyes of the Lord range throughout
the earth to strengthen those whose hearts
are fully committed to Him.*

2 CHRONICLES 16:9

This mentoring process—God as your life coach—can't really begin until it begins. We talked about trust back in chapter four. Now you need to take the next step and decide whether you are ready to commit to seeking God's best. Do you really want to know what the Bible says? Will you make the hard decisions this journey may require? Will you keep plowing through this guidebook written by a mere human with the goal of reaching new spiritual heights?

The chapters that follow will continue to be short and readable. But some of them will cover ground that may make you a little uncomfortable at first. So far your page turning and soul searching really hasn't been too painful, but that's about to change. This is where you either commit to going all the way or unceremoniously slide this book into a dusty bookshelf alongside all the other devotionals, Bible studies, and self-help books that really didn't help at all.

The good news is that your act of commitment will trigger a series of events that will bring new opportunities and open your eyes to new truths. A Scottish mountain climber and adventure writer from the last century, W. H. Murray, expresses this idea beautifully in *The Scottish Himalayan Expedition* (1951).

> The moment one definitely commits oneself, then Providence moves too. All sorts of things occur to help one that would never otherwise have occurred. A whole stream of events issue from the

decision, raising in one's favor all manner of unforeseen incidents and meetings and material assistance which no man could have dreamed would have come his way.

This is a big idea that should embolden any hesitant pilgrim. When you commit, the Creator of the Universe notices. He approves. And stands ready with a nudge, a boost, or a previously unknown revelation at just the right time.

Don't wait until the stars align perfectly to follow God's call on your life. Instead, take a bold first step and trust that God will direct a thousand more steps down a path chosen just for you. Along the way he may take you through dark tunnels and thorny passageways. But he will also give you courage, strength, and wisdom exactly when you need it. He will open hidden gates, provide unexpected resources, and introduce you to gifted strangers who will become best friends along the way.

The quote suggests that God moves. We know that's not true. He is an unshakeable rock, a firm foundation. But when we commit our life journey to him, his heart is moved. His strength overflows into your life as a new disciple. The verse from 2 Chronicles confirms that God is scanning the globe for people just like you. He promises to empower those who make a conscious decision to step out in faith.

10

Let's **step back**
and do a brief
self-assessment.

---

*Examine yourselves to see whether
you are in the faith; test yourselves.
Do you not realize that Christ Jesus is in you—
unless, of course, you fail the test?*

2 CORINTHIANS 13:5

In the course of your education, job hunting, and even volunteering, you may be subject to an occasional personality survey, character assessment, or psychoneurotic inventory. They include Myers-Briggs, DISC, and the Spirit-controlled temperament test designed by Dr. Tim LaHaye. You may have also seen a personality profile developed by Dr. Gary Smalley and Dr. John Trent that relates human characteristics to animals: lion, otter, golden retriever, and beaver. It's all fascinating stuff.

One of the great benefit of these assessments is the reminder that we're all different with our own strengths and weaknesses. That's true whether we're a strong-willed leader, enthusiastic friend, dependable peacemaker, or industrious organizer. On the other hand, one of the dangers of putting labels on individuals is that it may prevent you from—or give you an excuse for not—taking action. No matter what your label, when the world begins to crumble around you, you should dig deep and do whatever needs doing, whether it's offering compassion to launching a rescue operation.

For sure, assessment testing can be useful to an HR department or even to entrepreneurs who want to be aware of where they might invest their energies or what personal shortcoming may sidetrack their ambitions. But let's all agree not to allow anyone to force us to fill in some dots on a form and then corral us into some box that says, "You're only good for one thing."

Of course, God as your life coach is probably less concerned with your moneymaking career and more concerned about your moral character. So let's try a different kind of assessment. While the aforementioned temperament tests have no right or wrong answers, I hope you quickly see that this little self-quiz does.

- Are you quick to forgive or do you hold grudges?
- Can your words be trusted or do you cover your tracks with lies and excuses?
- Do you have a solid work ethic or expect others to provide for you?
- Can you delay gratification or do you need everything you want right now?
- Do you have well-considered convictions or do you let the situation determine what's right or wrong?
- Do you grimace and find fault when you look in a mirror or see a valuable child of God?
- Do you see people from all walks of life as valuable individuals or do you perpetuate stereotypes?
- Are you happy with your own stuff or do you drool over the neighbor's new purchases?
- Do you eat one more slice of pizza than you need or one less slice of pizza than you want?
- Do you toss candy wrappers out car windows or do you leave picnic areas cleaner than when you arrived?
- When given a task, do you follow through with excellence or do just enough to get by?

- Are people glad when you enter the room or when you exit the room?

Because God knows everything about you, this assessment wasn't for his benefit. It was for yours. I trust you don't feel too beat up by these dozen questions. Hopefully you did recognize a few areas in which you might improve. But not too many.

The point of this chapter is to embrace the truth that we all have room for improvement. That includes folks with multiple advanced degrees, folks who rescue puppies from burning buildings, folks who camp out at church day after day, and even folks who write books about having God as your life coach.

Let's see if the next chapter can help you identify some of the tools already at your disposal so you can start making those improvements.

11

What are your **resources**?
I've already given you a long list
of **useful gifts** and **talents**.

Each of you should use whatever gift
you have received to serve others,
as faithful stewards of God's grace
in its various forms.

1 PETER 4:10

One strategy for this chapter could be to leave these two pages blank and insist that you take an honest look at who you are and what you bring to the table. The goal would be to fill this space with stuff you do well or character traits that sparkle. You could start by shaking off any false humility and making a list of your own strengths off the top of your head. Then, you'd want to ask others who know you well and have seen you do great things or overcome insurmountable obstacles. Parents, teachers, coaches, pastors, friends, enemies, and so on.

Specifically, start by listing gifts you were born with. Then include life experiences that add a valuable layer to your personality, abilities, and motivations. Adversity you endured. Expertise learned by accident or necessity. Unexpected genius. Anything you might identify as a talent, flair, knack, or skill. And, again, that includes personality traits you had as a kid and those that have surfaced over the years.

For our purposes in this chapter, we're leaving out the bad stuff. For now, let's not dwell on your anger, fears, greed, guilt, and all those things that drag you down. This is a chapter focusing on the good stuff.

Below is by no means an exhaustive list, but it may trigger some ideas on how awesome you are. Honestly, how might you assess yourself? Circle as many as you can.

Empathetic	Enduring	Friendly	Thrifty
Calm	Decisive	Aware	Realistic
Sincere	Determined	Neat	Devoted

Joyful	Kind	Courageous	Logical
Loyal	Noble	Realistic	Sincere
Tolerant	Trustworthy	Warm	Decisive
Optimistic	Consistent	Outgoing	Poised
Inspiring	Capable	Ambitious	Clever
Analytical	Observant	Attentive	Balanced
Organized	Cautious	Certain	Scholarly
Charitable	Confident	Considerate	Diligent
Optimistic	Consistent	Outgoing	Patient
Cheerful	Conscientious	Courteous	Generous
Disciplined	Driven	Efficient	Practical
Grateful	Perceptive	Faithful	Focused
Graceful	Industrious	Enthusiastic	Flexible
Innovative	Modest	Nurturing	Obedient
Persevering	Professional	Punctual	Creative
Resourceful	Respectful	Responsible	Intelligent
Imaginative	Adventurous	Compassionate	

Now this list could backfire if you found only one or two words to circle. But that's probably not the case.

A good life coach will challenge you to take your positive traits and build on them. Another way to say that is *go with your strengths*. Identify those gifts and talents that are really clicking and use them to give back to God.

What happens if you choose not to partake in this exercise? Well, then there's no reason to get up in the morning, is there? Your work will never be as good as it could be. Your talent will be wasted. Your family and friends won't get the full benefit of whom you are. And God gets less glory.

What's more, never forget the list you've created with all those wonderful character traits really only scratches the surface. You are actually *much more* than that. Always remember, you were made in the image of God. Which means your gifts, talents, and potential are actually without limits.

12

I've also given you **strategies**
for using your personal resources
for good and noble purposes.

*For it is God who works in you to will
and to act in order to fulfill his good purpose.*

PHILIPPIANS 2:13

So you've got all this great stuff going for you. In the previous chapter, you circled more than a dozen positive and empowering character traits, and now you're ready to put them to use.

Just two thoughts before you proceed. First, please don't get too full of yourself, because those character traits technically were gifts from God. You are just a steward. Second, you still want to enlist God's help because what he has to offer multiplies the effectiveness of what you bring to the table a gazillion times over.

So how do you tap into God's guidance? Let's check Scripture. A pretty good plan for plugging directly into God's compass for your life begins with four proven, ancient strategies. Worship. Prayer. Wise counsel. The Bible itself.

- From John 4:23: But the time is coming—indeed it's here now—when true worshipers will worship the Father in spirit and in truth. The Father is looking for those who will worship him that way. (NLT)
- From Matthew 21:22: If you believe, you will receive whatever you ask for in prayer.
- From Proverbs 15:22: Plans fail for lack of counsel, but with many advisers they succeed.
- From Hebrews 4:12: For the word of God is alive and active. Sharper than any double-edged sword, it penetrates even to dividing soul and spirit, joints

and marrow; it judges the thoughts and attitudes of the heart.

Worship renews your mind so you can think clearly. Prayer opens God's heart. Wise advisers give you perspective you wouldn't have on your own. And the Bible is the guidebook that cuts through to the core of what really matters.

Overlook these four resources and you're setting yourself up for failure. That's where most human life coaches may fall way short. They spend so much time discerning the temperament and gifts of their individual clients, that they overlook the fact that our human contribution is the smallest piece of the puzzle.

Yes, you need to bring your best—no matter how meager it may seem—but it's God who commissions you to use it in ways you cannot imagine. Remember, this is the same God who designed the mustard seed. "Though it is the smallest of all seeds, yet when it grows, it is the largest of garden plants and becomes a tree, so that the birds come and perch in its branches" (Matthew 13:32).

Now that you've investigated four ways to actualize your gifts, let's consider a couple of reasons you may not be reaching your potential. Those two classic rationales: frustrations and excuses.

13

What are some of your current **frustrations**? There's often a reason I allow you to feel **a bit unsettled**.

Have I not commanded you?
Be strong and courageous.
Do not be terrified; do not be discouraged,
for the LORD your God will be
with you wherever you go.

JOSHUA 1:9

Funny things about frustrations. They are an excellent and accurate indicator of what's important to you.

Personally, I am not frustrated that the drapes in our living room don't match the pillows on the sofa. Or that my lawn has a few dandelions. Or that my receding hairline has finally joined forces with my bald spot. But I totally honor and respect my bride, Rita, who does care about a color-coordinated living space. I will not judge my neighbor who does obsess over his lawn. I will always be amazed that men spend thousands of dollars on hair transplants, weaves, and toupees.

What does frustrate me? Little things like typos and blocked emails. Also, slightly more critical issues such as keeping up with social media and meeting too-ambitious book deadlines. My biggest frustrations are probably universal to many Christians as we witness the disintegration of the family, the callous attitude toward life, and how mocking God's plan has become a cultural norm.

Can you see how identifying your frustrations reveals your passions and mission? Clearly I should not get a job as an interior designer, greenskeeper, or hair stylist. But as an author/speaker/family advocate/life pundit, I have found my sweet spot. Sitting at a keyboard or standing in front of an audience attempting to sort out the major issues of living a faith-filled life is precisely where I am supposed to be.

So what frustrates you? Whatever it is, don't allow it to become an excuse for inaction or gridlock in your life.

Instead, rejoice in it. Because you may have uncovered what's important to you. And that's where you might make your biggest impact on the world.

In 2 Corinthians, Paul famously describes and ruminates over his unspecified "thorn in the flesh." It was a weakness quite frustrating to him. But he saw value in that shortcoming, whatever it was. It kept him humble, focused on his task, and dependent on God.

> In order to keep me from becoming conceited, I was given a thorn in my flesh, a messenger of Satan, to torment me. Three times I pleaded with the Lord to take it away from me. But he said to me, "My grace is sufficient for you, for my power is made perfect in weakness." Therefore I will boast all the more gladly about my weaknesses, so that Christ's power may rest on me. That is why, for Christ's sake, I delight in weaknesses, in insults, in hardships, in persecutions, in difficulties. For when I am weak, then I am strong. (2 Corinthians 12:7-10)

Typically if a human life coach says, "You need to depend on me alone," you'll want to run far, far away. But when God says it, you can believe him. His grace is sufficient. His power shows up when we acknowledge our dependence on him. When we are frustrated, broken, and weak, he is strong.

14

What's your
favorite excuse?

*The man said, "The woman you put here with me—
she gave me some fruit from the tree, and I ate it."*

GENESIS 3:12

Let's take a moment for a brief rant. One of the great failures of the next generation might be that no one wants to take responsibility for their actions. Excuses come easy. And they often include a side order of whining.

It's not a new problem. Making excuses for a bad choice was pivotal to the sequence of events surrounding the first sin. Imagine Adam in the Garden of Eden. His new bride offers him fruit from the forbidden tree and, without much thought, he takes a big old bite. When confronted by the Creator, Adam whines that it's not his fault. He even insinuates it's God's fault! He blames it on "the woman you put here with me."

The first couple disobeyed God and then lied to God, but it's the whining and blaming someone else that put the final nail in their coffin. Adam and Eve were not alone in their excuse-making. Here are three more whine-filled excuses from Scripture.

Proverbs 22:13 offers a silly-sounding evasion of responsibility that demonstrates how most excuses have an air of foolishness: "The sluggard says, 'There's a lion outside! I'll be killed in the public square!'" Really, a lion? You're not going to work because there's a lion outside? Or maybe—as your name suggests—you're just a slug.

In the Parable of the Talents, two investors earned a profit on the money provided by the master. But the third man didn't want to risk losing the money. He let fear be his excuse. He whined, "So I was afraid and went out and hid your gold in the ground. See, here is what belongs to you" (Matthew 25:25). A few verses later we learned that excuse-maker was tossed out into the darkness, weeping and gnashing his teeth.

One surprising excuse maker is Moses. Early in Exodus, Moses is holding an actual conversation with God himself. God has already showed him a nifty batch of miracles and then instructs Moses to be his spokesman to Pharaoh. Moses has the chutzpah to reply, "Pardon your servant, Lord. I have never been eloquent, neither in the past nor since you have spoken to your servant. I am slow of speech and tongue" (Exodus 4:10).

Making excuses is a common human trait. Some are even justifiable. As your life coach, God will certainly acknowledge and assist you with any legitimate concerns or challenges holding you back. But he's also in the business of brushing excuses aside. He's waiting to give you victory. Romans 8:37 promises, "We are more than conquerors through him who loved us."

So let's pledge to spend less time looking for reasons to fail and more time looking for reasons to claim victory. As George Washington Carver said, "Ninety-nine percent of the failures come from people who have the habit of making excuses."

15

Allow me to make some observations.
I see all of time and space.
And I promise you,
the plan works.

Nothing in all creation is hidden from God's sight.
Everything is uncovered and laid bare before the eyes
of him to whom we must give account.

HEBREWS 4:13

The view that God has is not the view that you and I have. For now, he has limited our vision. That's a good thing because honestly, we can only handle so much. Great joys and great sorrows lie ahead for all of us. They come in a flash and impact us forever. If we saw the big picture and knew everything that waited around the next corner, it would blow our minds. We'd run for cover or freeze in our tracks.

Still, we can trust God because he has an eternal perspective. He sees all of time and space in the same instant. And it all works out. The best-known verse reflecting that idea is Romans 8:28: "God causes everything to work together for the good of those who love God and are called according to His purpose for them."

Accepting that truth is a spiritual discipline. It requires us to trust God to take the sum of all our experiences and use them for good. That's a theme that arches over the entire Bible—God's promise of deliverance from darkness to light. From being lost to being found.

Authentic Christians will instantly recognize that God's plan culminates in our spending eternity with him. They know life on earth is a blink compared to our eternal destination. God has prepared a place for us and we're not home yet.

But there's a second dimension to God's promise of deliverance. The Bible tells us that following God offers double value—purpose in this life and security in the next. "Godliness is profitable for all things, since it holds promise for the present life and *also* for the *life* to come" (1 Timothy 4:8 NASB).

In other words, with God as your life coach, he will guide you into eternity *and* your life on earth finally makes sense. The joys of life are deeper because it's not just about you. You realize things like beauty, love, freedom, friendship, hope, and life itself are really gifts from the Creator. You have a relationship with God and other believers. What's more, the frustrations of life on earth—even the horrors—are filtered through a lens of confidence knowing that God will use them somehow for good.

Put another way, our heavenly Father looks down and sees all time and space—past, present and future—at the same instant. He sees the Garden of Eden, the Garden of Gethsemane, and the herb garden in your backyard. At this very moment, God sees your first cries as a newborn, he sees that difficult day one of your dreams was crushed and you cursed him, and he sees the remarkable day when you cross from this life into eternity. Being part of that intentional plan should give you overflowing hope and assurance.

So, again, it comes down to trust. As we move into the core of this book, your job is to let God speak to your heart through some universal truths. Truths that are true for everyone. But feel free to own them as your own.

16

You're **normal.**
But I've given you everything
you need to be **so much more.**

*No temptation has overtaken you
except what is common to mankind.*

1 CORINTHIANS 10:13

I hate to break it to you. But all the stuff you're going through is typical of humans all over the world. The good stuff. The bad stuff. The tedious stuff. The stuff that makes it worth getting up in the morning.

You may feel like no one else has ever been cut from a basketball team. You may feel like no one else has ever lost their job, had their lunch stolen from the company fridge, or suffered a paper cut. You may think your watercolor is worthy of the Guggenheim. You may think your recipe for three-bean salad is the most delish ever. The truth is we all have highs and lows. We are all in the same boat. We all need food, oxygen, warmth, and human contact. We all have limited time on this planet. We all have sinned and fall short of the glory of God (Romans 3:23).

That's right. You're not special at all.

If that sounds a little harsh, my apologies. It's just that there are way too many people out there—not necessarily you—who think way too highly of themselves. They think the world owes them some kind of special privileges. They mistakenly believe they are the center of the universe. Why does that happen? Maybe life has been too easy for too long. Their mommy picked up their clothes. Their daddy never had them do chores. Maybe they are just so beautiful or so clever that the world around them simply falls at their feet. These individuals would never describe themselves as normal.

Well, welcome to reality. And I hope you're not too ticked off about being lumped in with all the rest of us schmucks.

With that understanding, I can confirm that being human is not all bad. You were created in God's image (Genesis 1:27). You have dominion over birds, fish, and all the animals (Genesis 1:26). You were fearfully and wonderfully made (Psalm 139:14).

If normal is not what you want to be, then there are things you can do to set yourself apart. But be warned, those endeavors may require you to step outside your comfort zone. Consider a day volunteering in a food kitchen. An overnight visiting the urban homeless. An afternoon doing prison visitations. A week babysitting your neighbor's toddler while she's in the hospital. An exhausting, eye-opening ten-day mission trip. Dropping a sizable anonymous gift in the Salvation Army kettle. Sidewalk counseling outside a Planned Parenthood clinic. Delivering an Angel Tree gift to the children of an inmate. Or any other opportunity to serve that God puts on your heart.

In Matthew 20:26-28, Jesus explains greatness, "Whoever wants to become great among you must be your servant, and whoever wants to be first must be your slave—just as the Son of Man did not come to be served, but to serve, and to give his life as a ransom for many."

Exhibiting the heart and mind of a servant can actually turn normal people into great people. So go for it.

17

You're **exceptional.**
But that means I will be expecting
much from you.

O Lord, you have examined my heart and know
everything about me. You know when I sit down or stand up.
You know my thoughts even when I'm far away. You see me
when I travel and when I rest at home. You know everything
I do. You know what I am going to say even before I say it,
LORD. You go before me and follow me. You place your hand
of blessing on my head. Such knowledge is too wonderful
for me, too great for me to understand!

PSALM 139:1-6 NLT

You know that last chapter? The chapter that insisted you were just one of seven billion people on the planet who are all pretty much the same? I take it all back.

You are unique. You are extraordinary. You are wonderfully wonderful.

The Creator of the universe knows you, cares about you, and follows your every move. Even before you say something, he knows what you're going to say. This idea is impossible to comprehend, but God leads you and God follows you. And you're worth it. As your life coach, he would be the first to tell you that he doesn't waste his time on people and projects that are dead ends.

That's right. You're one of God's favorites. And he has big plans for you.

If that seems like a lot of pressure, my apologies. It's just that there are way too many people out there—not necessarily you—who have no idea how fabulous and valuable they are. They trudge through life discouraged or embittered in the belief they have no purpose. Why does that happen? Perhaps they experienced physical or emotional abuse as a child. Mom didn't hold them. Dad was too busy or too brutal. Maybe no one ever told them they were loved by God. Maybe they are just so filled with fear, depression, and anxiety that they see no hope for the future. They would never consider themselves to be exceptional.

If that describes you in even the slightest, welcome to your new reality. You have more to offer than you can ever imagine. Special powers. The power to love, give, weep, smile, heal, encourage, instruct, comfort, and so much more.

Where should you invest and engage these powers for the most good? You could travel to the other side of the planet, but you don't have to. Within minutes of your home, there's work to be done. Be warned, these endeavors may require you to step outside your comfort zone. But worry not; you have everything you need.

(As it turns out, the opportunities before you are the exact same opportunities presented in the previous chapter to those who think too highly of themselves. In both cases, it's all about serving God by serving others.)

Consider a day volunteering in a food kitchen. An overnight visiting the urban homeless. An afternoon doing prison visitations. A week babysitting your neighbor's toddler while she's in the hospital. An exhausting, eye-opening ten-day mission trip. Dropping a sizable anonymous gift in the Salvation Army kettle. Sidewalk counseling outside a Planned Parenthood clinic. Delivering an Angel Tree gift to the children of an inmate. Or any other opportunity to serve God puts on your heart.

In Luke 12:48, Jesus explains your responsibility as an exceptional person: "From everyone who has been given much, much will be demanded; and from the one who has been entrusted with much, much more will be asked."

You have been given much. I hope you realize that. But don't think too highly of yourself. No matter what, you're still a little lower than the angels (Hebrews 2:7).

18

You're **doing** a lot
of things **right**.

Do your best to present yourself to God as one approved,
a worker who does not need to be ashamed
and who correctly handles the word of truth.

2 TIMOTHY 2:15

Don't you love Bible verses that let you off the hook with phrases that take pressure off rather than heap on more guilt and incrimination.

You have to admit there are all kinds of commands and demands in Scripture that seem almost impossible. Love your enemy (Matthew 5:44). Thou shalt not covet (Romans 13:9). Be patient toward all men (1 Thessalonians 5:14).

Then, of course, there's this truly impossible instruction from Matthew 5:48: "Be perfect, therefore, as your heavenly Father is perfect." Theologians suggest that this verse is really a challenge to grow in our pursuit of perfection. It also provides a glimpse into our heavenly future where we will be perfected.

I think most people will agree that many of the expectations found in the Bible can be a bit overwhelming to mere mortals. Thankfully, there are verses like 1 Timothy 2:15. It tosses out the challenge to never be ashamed of the Gospel, to live in the light of God's truth, and to seek God's approval. But it begins with words, "Do your best . . ."

Phew. That sounds more doable. *All I have to do is my best. That's a choice I can make. I can't choose to do the impossible. But I can choose to set my priorities, dig deep, and refuse to give him anything less than he deserves.*

Does that verse really "let you off the hook"? Of course not. It's an unmistakable reminder that our goal is to do our very best. No matter what.

I'm recalling the season of my life when I left a high-profile advertising agency in Chicago to begin a career in radio production and marketing for Christian publishers and ministries. As you can imagine, after working with nationally known brands, suddenly my media and production budgets were dramatically lower. So were expectations from clients. Integrity and biblical values were given much higher priority than creativity and attention to detail. For a brief period I got caught up in the tragic mindset that we couldn't afford excellence, nor was it necessary. Thankfully, I shook off that attitude and committed to pursuing innovation and fresh vision on behalf of my clients in Christian media. That's also when I realized why God had me spend that time as a Michigan Avenue creative. He wanted my best efforts—which included the practices and strategies sharpened at downtown ad agencies—to be used for his glory.

God deserves our best. Even with smaller budgets and fewer staff.

Maybe you can relate to the Little Drummer Boy singing, "I have no gifts to bring . . . (but) I'll play my best for him."

So, what's your best right now? Here's a hint. It's about surrendering and pursuing. Committing to commitment. Being willing to examine yourself and admit your fears and failures. Making fewer excuses and taking full responsibility.

So consider this chapter a pat on the back. Keep doing your best. You're going to fall short. But you're also going to do more than you ever thought possible. Pa-rum-pa-pum-pum.

19

You already have
everything you need
to be everything you want.
I guarantee it.

His divine power has given us everything we need
for a godly life through our knowledge of him
who called us by his own glory and goodness.

2 PETER 1:3

Here's a big secret the life coaching fraternity doesn't want you to know. With a new client, they generally spend the first several sessions asking questions, completing surveys, and mapping personality traits. All the while they are listening for clues and reading between the lines to assess their client's unspoken hopes and dreams.

The pretext is that the life coach is scientifically determining the skills and experiences of a client in order to identify and help the client navigate the path to certain future success. But that's an overstatement. Really, no test would ever reveal that information. However, with the right prompting and careful listening, a life coach can eventually uncover the client's secret yearnings of the heart.

It may take five or six sessions. That's when you can pretty much count on the big reveal. "Wow!" they will say, "I've been a life coach for many years, but never before have I seen such a clear path for a client to reach their untapped potential. Your success indicators are off the charts! I'm so excited for you."

Then the life coach simply repeats back to the unsuspecting client one of the fantasy scenarios that were revealed over the previous weeks.

- "You are supposed to open a restaurant."
- "Do whatever it takes to get your MBA."
- "You need to actively pursue speaking engagements with major corporations so that the world can gain access to your insight."

- "You have the heart and soul of an artist. You will find success and fulfillment as soon as you surrender to your artistic giftedness."

Such suggestions might actually be the exact right advice for their client. More than likely, it's something they've been wanting to do for years, and they are delighted to have the confirmation of a life coaching professional. The big reveal and bold declaration becomes the kick in the pants they needed. In many ways, I endorse their tactic.

Now, if all this sounds a bit cynical, I apologize. But really, what else can a human life coach do? His job is to find a way to encourage their clients to pursue their dreams.

With God as your life coach, it's actually much easier. You don't have to reinvent yourself. You don't have to quit your job and travel to some distant mountain in search of the meaning life. You don't even have to talk to a life coach for six very expensive two-hour sessions. Instead, just do what's right in front of you with excellence, perseverance, and a smile on your face. Ecclesiastes 9:10 says, "Whatever your hand finds to do, do it with all your might."

What does that do? you ponder. *How does performing mundane chores with excellence open new vistas of opportunity and help me harvest all my gifts?*

Well keep reading, friend. You'll see those routine chores aren't routine at all. But first, we've got some obstacles to clear, gifts to accept, work to do, and big plans to reveal.

20

But there are **obstacles**.
And, yes, there is a reason I allow you
to **stumble** once in a while.

Consider it pure joy, my brothers and sisters,
whenever you face trials of many kinds,
because you know that the testing of your faith
produces perseverance. Let perseverance finish
its work so that you may be mature and complete,
not lacking anything.

JAMES 1:2-4

I know you're eager to graduate from these boring early chapters and finally uncover your fresh and progressive way of looking at life. The shiny new you. That's the magic promise you expect when you sign on with a life coach, right? Well, hold on. There are some cobwebs, stumbling blocks, and garbage to deal with beforehand.

You knew that, but you just didn't want to think about it. Or maybe you're in denial.

Some of these obstacles are self-inflicted. A bad choice that left some scars. A small irritation that became a major hassle because you chose to ignore it. One of the Ten Commandments you read, understood, and thought didn't apply to you.

Some of these obstacles are simply a part of life in this broken world. A fear or insecurity left over from childhood. The distractions and vanities of the world that are meaningless, yet steal the attention of so many people. Or maybe you think you've got your act together and already have a golden ticket to easy street. Be warned, that fast track you think you're on is really an impassable obstacle you will never conquer on your own.

What does a wise person do with obstacles? Identify them. And make them work *in your favor*.

Read again that remarkable passage from James 1. Consider trials to be pure joy. They test you, revealing where you need to put in a little extra work. They sharpen and strengthen you. They help you appreciate the power of perseverance. I'm not 100 percent sure about the accuracy of the quote, "What doesn't kill you makes you stronger," but there's at least a hint of truth there.

Obstacles and trials will test you to see where you put your faith. Is it in yourself? Is it in your bank account and the contents of your safe deposit box? Does your faith depend on your Dunlop Grand Slam racket when you're down two sets to one or your Miken Rain carbon fiber bat when you're facing the best pitcher in the league?

Well you *should* develop a modest degree of self-confidence. A healthy bank balance is a good thing. It allows you to be generous and take advantage of opportunities that God places in your life. Once you reach a certain level of sports involvement, you should resource yourself with the best equipment you can find. But, don't put your faith in deep pockets or expensive gadgets.

By facing obstacles, you will gain maturity, perseverance, and integrity. You're putting your faith to the test. But the faith you're developing is not in yourself or worldly possessions. The faith you're developing . . . is in faith. Faith in God's love and purpose for your life.

Let's spend the next few chapters wrestling with some of these frustrating, but potentially valuable obstacles. Some you'll identify with more than others. But don't skip any. Just in case.

21

Are you **caught**
in the grip of **fear**?

*What does the Lord your God ask of you but to fear
the Lord your God, to walk in obedience to him,
to love him, to serve the Lord your God
with all your heart and with all your soul.*

DEUTERONOMY 10:12

It's been suggested that one of the main reasons individuals seek out a life coach is not so much to achieve greatness as to overcome a fear. Perhaps they're hanging on to some phobia they think might be holding them back from success. Atychiphobia. Glossophobia. Agoraphobia. Which, you may know, is fear of failure, fear of public speaking, and fear of open spaces or crowds. Add to that the fear of rejection, fear of commitment, or even fear of success, and you'll see why there's a legitimate market for life coaching.

Fear is a universal obstacle. I have a sense that all of us suffer from some level of intimidation or hesitation when facing the challenges of life. We get tongue-tied on a speaking platform. We don't want to appear foolish. We want to make our parents proud. We're afraid to share hopes and dreams because some naysayer may laugh at our idea.

In my early teens, just for fun, I recorded my voice into a cassette player pretending to be a disc jockey introducing songs. A few days later, my older brother heard the tape and mocked my efforts. (Something you would certainly expect from a big brother.) Fear of any further ridicule may have stalled my radio career for about three decades.

I also know at least three friends who didn't follow through on solid ideas for new businesses. Maybe it was money or marketplace holding them back. But after talking with them, I have a sense that fear definitely played a part.

Now, the kinds of fears we're talking about in this chapter are not the natural or instinctual fear of snakes, spiders, high places, cancer, or thunderstorms. After all, those things can kill ya. We're talking about the fear of things that are keeping you from your best life.

The good news is that there exists a fear that can actually *help* you overcome your other fears. The fear of God. Don't think of it as a phobia, but rather the attitude of approaching God with absolute awe, respect, and reverence. Just the thought of God should be so stunning that we are blown away when he freely offers us love, grace, and forgiveness.

What's more, once we accept God's love, fear should have no hold on us. Our purpose and place in eternity is secure. And nothing can separate us from the love of God. The Bible teaches, "There is no fear in love. But perfect love casts out fear" (1 John 4:18).

Perfect unconditional love—which only God can give—can free you and me to be our best. From an eternal perspective, we never have to be afraid of anything ever again. Not death. Not insignificance. Not Satan. Not even fear of a little teasing by an older brother.

22

Is envy stirring
dissatisfaction
with your life?

A heart at peace gives life to the body,
but envy rots the bones.

PROVERBS 14:30

Have you heard Aesop's fable on the inevitable self-destruction that comes from being envious?

A good-hearted butcher throws a good-sized bone to a little dog that hurries home with his prize. Crossing a narrow footbridge, he looks down into the still water and sees another dog with an even bigger bone. Or so he thinks. The first dog barks at the rival dog and jumps into the water. The one and only bone sinks to the bottom and the little dog paddles grimly to the riverbank. Feeling a little foolish he shakes himself damp and continues home muddy and boneless.

That's envy. You've got something pretty good. A home. A bed. A car. A spouse. But you want the version that's bigger, softer, faster, or better looking.

What happens then? How does envy almost always end up? Most of the time, it's just wishful thinking that distracts you from appreciating what you already have. That's tragic enough. But often envy is destructive and soul crushing to all involved.

Consider the homeowner envious of his neighbor's house with the three-car garage and the extra bedroom. Every time he pulls in his driveway, he's bitter. When he walks in the door with that attitude, his family suffers. Household chores and maintenance on his "shack" become woeful burdens. Worse, envy incites the man to buy a bigger house he can't afford and his financial security crumbles.

The individual coveting a new mattress or new car needs to spend a bit more time considering the homeless person sleeping under the viaduct or waiting for a city bus in the rain.

Then, of course, how many marriages dissolve because of some version of envy? A wife or husband notices the way another couple appears to be lovey-dovey and super supportive of each other. What that envious individual sees may be real or an illusion. Either way, an obsession begins. And precious time and effort is wasted fixating on the other couple's perfect marriage.

Here's the point. Envy steals time, energy, creativity, and hope. Every moment spent craving something we don't have steals time we should be investing in our own resources and relationships.

There will always be someone with a bigger house, so take care of your own home and let them worry about security systems and cleaning extra bathrooms. There will always be someone with better toys, but toys lose their appeal and end up broken or forgotten.

Thanks to health clubs, glossy magazines, and cosmetic surgeons, there will always be men and women more beautiful then your spouse. No, I take that back. Your husband or wife is perfectly, wonderfully beautiful, if you take envy out of the equation.

As for Aesop's bone-less dog? I hope he learned his lesson to be happy with what he already has.

23

What triggers your
anger?

Take note of this: Everyone should be quick to listen,
slow to speak and slow to become angry,
because human anger does not produce
the righteousness that God desires.

JAMES 1:19-20

Do you ever find yourself in the middle of a reckless rage, and then make it worse by coming up with excuses and rationalizations? You may even argue that anger itself is not a moral issue by pointing out that even Jesus got angry when he overturned the tables of the money-changers in the temple.

Well, you are partially correct. But there's more to the story. It's imperative to differentiate between righteous anger and selfish anger. Righteous anger is what Jesus modeled in Matthew 21. He didn't lose control. He saw the desecration of the temple, quoted the prophet Isaiah, and delivered a clear message, "It is written," he said to them, "'My house will be called a 'house of prayer,' but you are making it 'a den of robbers.'"

Righteous anger and controlled resolve are the proper response to such evils as child abuse, racism, abortion, and other injustices. But selfish anger is often out of control. Have you ever gotten mad at someone who messed up, but it was a complete accident and they already feel terrible about it? Or how about losing your temper with a young child or a puppy? Then there are the ridiculous times you cursed at a vending machine or kitchen appliance. Uncontrolled, selfish anger leads you down a path you don't want to go. Psalm 37:8 says, "Refrain from anger and turn from wrath; do not fret—it leads only to evil.

There are not many feelings worse than raging uncontrollably at someone you love. Don't you wish there was a way to turn aside those impulses that trigger your angry response? Might it be possible to eliminate selfish anger all together? I don't think we can. The Bible also says, "In your anger do not sin" (Ephesians 4:26). That seems to suggest that anger may be part of human nature, but it's what we do with our anger that makes all the difference.

As your life coach, God might suggest that the way to control anger is to slow down. To lengthen the fuse. That gives you a chance to consider the real cause of the anger, determine whether it really deserves such an explosion, and to recognize who's in our direct line of fire. It may sound cliché, but counting to ten before letting loose may be a prudent exercise.

The best reason to be slow to anger is because it allows us time to consider the bigger picture. Maybe the experience or event causing your anger is actually part of God's bigger plan for your life that has not yet been revealed. We get angry when our home loan is turned down, but it saves us from buying a house on an unidentified flood plain. We get angry when our daughter's heart is broken by her jerk of a boyfriend, but she may very soon meet the love of her life. We get angry when we miss that promotion, but the new job would have meant double the workload for a tyrannical boss. This is all stuff God knows, but we don't.

There's a fable about a man shipwrecked on a desert island. Already miserable, the man's primitive bamboo hut is destroyed by a bolt of lightning. He angrily shakes his fist at God, but an hour later, a passing ship rescues him. The captain says, "We came because we saw your smoke signals."

Our explosive outrage at frustrating situations is really an indication that we don't accept God's plan. For sure, anger is a natural human emotion. But, sometime in the near future, you'll need to decide whether or not you're going to surrender to the idea that God's long-range, big picture perspective is worthy of your trust.

24

Having doubts?
Let's get them out
in the open.

If any of you lacks wisdom, you should ask God,
who gives generously to all without finding fault,
and it will be given to you. But when you ask,
you must believe and not doubt, because the one
who doubts is like a wave of the sea,
blown and tossed by the wind.

JAMES 1:5-6

You know the story of Doubting Thomas, but allow me to set the scene. Several days after the crucifixion, rumors were spreading that Jesus of Nazareth had risen from the dead. All but one of his disciples had actually seen the risen Christ and some were beginning to feel empowered enough to make such an outrageous claim public. That's where John 20:24-29 begins.

> One of the twelve disciples, Thomas (nicknamed the Twin), was not with the others when Jesus came. They told him, "We have seen the Lord!" But he replied, "I won't believe it unless I see the nail wounds in his hands, put my fingers into them, and place my hand into the wound in his side." Eight days later the disciples were together again, and this time Thomas was with them. The doors were locked; but suddenly, as before, Jesus was standing among them. "Peace be with you," he said. Then he said to Thomas, "Put your finger here, and look at my hands. Put your hand into the wound in my side. Don't be faithless any longer. Believe!" "My Lord and my God!" Thomas exclaimed. Then Jesus told him, "You believe because you have seen me. Blessed are those who believe without seeing me." (NLT)

A few things are worth pointing out here. Thomas was just being honest. He's a guy who needs solid evidence, which is not a bad trait. Healthy skepticism can inspire you to do a little research, which ultimately strengthens your argument when someone challenges what you believe. Also note that Jesus didn't chastise Thomas. He told him to be at peace and then gave Thomas the proof he needed. Doubt didn't keep Thomas from that locked upper room. Doubt led him to clarify his position and seek the facts.

So let's do the same with any doubts you may have. Do you doubt your ability to finish this book? Well, the facts are that you are more than a third of the way through, and future chapters don't suddenly show up in Mandarin or invisible ink. So you're on the right track.

Do you doubt your ability to hear or recognize God's direction for your life? You're not alone. But Proverbs 16:3 does promise, "Commit to the Lord whatever you do, and he will establish your plans."

Do you doubt the existence of God? Your life coach, of course, might chuckle and say, "I'm right here." But then he might challenge you to identify the source of your uncertainty. Many people tend to look for reasons *not* to believe, when the truth is right in front of them. Romans 10:17 provides one sure answer: "Faith comes from hearing the message, and the message is heard through the word about Christ."

Embrace your doubts. Define them. Seek truth. Like Thomas, go ahead and share your doubts with people you trust.

One final note on doubt. Since there is no other mention of a twin brother, theologians aren't exactly sure why the Bible tells us of Thomas' nickname. Who and where is that doubting twin? I have a hunch it might be me. Or you.

25

Laziness is not part of my plan for your life.

We do not want you to become lazy,
but to imitate those who through faith
and patience inherit what has been promised.

HEBREWS 6:12

Yes, I have written a lot of books and produced thousands of radio spots and programs, and I've been paying my bills mostly on time for the last thirty years. But I confess that—more than I care to admit—I am occasionally, mournfully sloth-like.

So in honor of my laziness, I'm going to let God write most of the remainder of this chapter. It turns out that the Bible, and especially the book of Proverbs, has quite a bit to say about idle hands, sluggards, and those unwilling to work.

> A sluggard's appetite is never filled, but the desires of the diligent are fully satisfied. (Proverbs 13:4)

> Do not love sleep or you will grow poor; stay awake and you will have food to spare. (Proverbs 20:13)

> Through laziness, the rafters sag; because of idle hands, the house leaks. (Ecclesiastes 10:18)

> Work hard and become a leader; be lazy and become a slave. (Proverbs 12:24 NLT)

> The one who is unwilling to work shall not eat. (2 Thessalonians 3:10)

> As a door turns on its hinges, so a sluggard turns on his bed. (Proverbs 26:14)

Lazy people irritate their employers, like vinegar to the teeth or smoke in the eyes. (Proverbs 10:26–27 NLT)

The lazy do not roast any game, but the diligent feed on the riches of the hunt. (Proverbs 12:27)

Did you get all that? You may think that lazy people just eat, sleep, and muddle through life facing very low expectations from others. But go back and read these eight short passages again.

The truth is that lazy people irritate their bosses, have leaky roofs, never get a good night's sleep, and don't get much to eat. They even miss out on the family barbecue because they chose not to participate in the hunt. Often, being lazy just makes more work, which is totally counterproductive.

So how do I overcome my own propensity toward laziness? Here are my three secrets.

1. Don't be a loner. Surround yourself with people interdependent on each other. Often that's family. But it could be a circle of close friends that challenge each other to realize their destinies. It can be difficult to motivate yourself just for yourself. But when people you care about need you to get out and hustle, that can be a daily spark to get your engine going.

2. Set deadlines. Often the only reason I drag my sorry self out of bed is because I have a specific, looming deadline set by a client or publisher. But *self-imposed* deadlines and quotas can also do the trick. Deadlines such as wallpapering the dining room before Thanksgiving. Raking the leaves before the first snowfall of the season. Communicating with five human resource departments by three p.m. on Thursday. Selling twenty cases by Friday. Writing 2,000 words a day for the entire month of April. (Suddenly you've completed a 60,000-word book.) The goal with deadlines is not to set yourself up for failure. It's simply to bite off exactly what you can chew.

3. Acknowledge your gifts. There are many, many things I do not do well. I will not list them here. Nor do I dwell on them. Nor do I call myself lazy when I refuse to do them. But there are some ways in which I have been gifted and I need to be faithful with those gifts. It's only fair. Since I have let myself slide in areas at which other people do so much better than me, I figure I need to do what I can do. Right?

Finally, one of the key reasons I can't afford to be lazy is that I am kind of looking forward to God someday saying to me, "Well done, good and faithful servant" (Matthew 25:21).

26

Where do you turn
for security?
(I'm right here.)

He lifted me out of the slimy pit,
out of the mud and mire;
he set my feet on a rock
and gave me a firm place to stand.

PSALM 40:2

Following Jesus is risky business. You can't look back. You've got to step out in faith. You might have to make radical changes to your life. Maybe you're not a risk taker. Small changes bother you. Big changes freak you out. You like security.

I get it. You're not alone with those thoughts and emotions. Below are three brief examples of individuals who were considering following Jesus and didn't quite get it right.

In Luke 9, we read about a dude who actually had the audacity to tell Jesus to wait. Jesus himself is drafting disciples. One recruit says, "Yes, Lord, I will follow you, but first let me say good-bye to my family." Jesus doesn't pull any punches. He says, "Anyone who puts a hand to the plow and then looks back is not fit for the Kingdom of God" (Luke 9:61-62 NLT).

Does that sound a little mean? No. It's just honest. Once you decide to follow Jesus, keep your eyes on him. Put Christ ahead of everything—even your family. And frankly, there's no reason to look back. God is in control. He will take care of everything that really matters.

In Matthew 14, Jesus surprises the disciples by walking across the waves toward their boat. They think he's a ghost, but he tells them not to be afraid. Peter, who often seems to go a little overboard, calls out, "Lord, if it's you, tell me to come to you on the water." "'Come,' he said. Then Peter got down out of the boat, walked on the water and came toward Jesus" (Matthew 14:28-29).

It's a pretty amazing moment. But then Peter notices the wind, takes his eyes off Jesus, and begins to sink. It turns out Peter likes the security of actually being in a boat when he finds himself in the middle of the Sea of Galilee.

In Mark 10, a well-meaning rich young man comes to Jesus. "'Good teacher,' he asked, 'what must I do to inherit eternal life?'" After some conversation about following the commandments, Jesus finally says, "'One thing you lack. Go, sell everything you have and give to the poor, and you will have treasure in heaven. Then come, follow me.' At this the man's face fell. He went away sad, because he had great wealth" (Mark 10:17, 21-22).

These men thought security was found in family, in a sturdy boat, or in financial wealth. They would be wrong. God as your life coach would confirm that pursuing life from a solid, secure location is a great idea. But most of life is a slimy, miry, muddy pit. You need to set your feet on the rock. That's your best—and really only—firm foundation.

27

I have a **plan** for **any** and all insurmountable **obstacles.**

The LORD will fight for you;
you need only to be still.

EXODUS 14:14

Once in a while, a life coach may have a client with an obstacle that is insurmountable. A predicament that seems unsolvable. Maybe they are caught between a rock and a hard place. Or caught between a wide sea and a swiftly approaching army of chariots and horsemen.

Such was the case of the Israelites in the early days of their Exodus from Egypt. They had no place to go and thought they were done for.

> As Pharaoh approached, the Israelites looked up, and there were the Egyptians, marching after them. They were terrified and cried out to the LORD. They said to Moses, "Was it because there were no graves in Egypt that you brought us to the desert to die? What have you done to us by bringing us out of Egypt? Didn't we say to you in Egypt, 'Leave us alone; let us serve the Egyptians'? It would have been better for us to serve the Egyptians than to die in the desert!" (Exodus 14:10-12)

Sure, they were in a tough spot. But instead of whining, the Israelites should have known better. They had already survived ten nasty plagues in Egypt including the slaughter of all the firstborn Egyptian sons. God had been clearly leading them with a pillar of fire by night and pillar of cloud by day. Their leader, Moses, had even been in direct communication with God. Still, they whined that slavery was better than this dilemma.

In response, Moses—who trusted God but had no idea what to do next—delivered the line we should all remember when we're stuck between that rock and hard place. "The LORD will fight for you; you need only to be still."

The best way to overcome an insurmountable obstacle is to do less whining and more listening. God will fight on your behalf. He has a plan for you. Expect it. Count on it.

Two things to remember. First, God's response may be totally surprising. For the Israelites, it was parting the Red Sea. For you, it may be closing a huge door or opening a new window. It may be restoring something broken or breaking something unbreakable. It may be sending you a rescuer in the form of an invincible angel, discerning mentor, soft-spoken child, or candid truth-teller. Honestly, you might not like the sound of God's plan. In that case, a little trust will go along way.

Second, you will likely be called to action. At the edge of the Red Sea, with the entire Egyptian army thundering in the Israelites' direction, Moses was instructed to raise his staff and the Israelites were instructed to travel through the dry seabed.

Our willingness to participate in God's plan builds our faith and convictions. He doesn't need our help, but we need to partner with him for our own spiritual well being.

Best of all, seeing God rescue us from insurmountable obstacles gives us stories to tell of how he works in the lives of real people who seek his favor. Those stories are what makes the Bible such a compelling and inspiring book.

28

Beware of the slippery slope.

This is what the wicked are like—always free of care . . .
Surely you place them on slippery ground;
you cast them down to ruin.
How suddenly are they destroyed,
completely swept away by terrors!

PSALM 73:12, 18-19

One of the great obstacles to engaging God as your life coach is not an obstacle at all. It's the slippery slope that can have us moving too fast and too far down a steep decline that takes us further and farther away from his best plans for us.

Examples of the slippery slope are easy to find. Church bingo leads to a state run lottery, which leads to a plethora of casinos. An innocent flirtation leads to a long lunch, which leads to a marriage-destroying affair. Vulgar language leads to even more vulgar language. And so on.

I know you're basically a good person doing the best you can. But what most folks don't realize is how easily one teeny, tiny bad decision leads to another. In C. S. Lewis' memorable book, *The Screwtape Letters*, the diabolical elder demon pens some wise advice to his apprentice advocating the effectiveness of the slippery slope. Uncle Screwtape writes, "The safest road to Hell is the gradual one. This is the road taken by quiet people, responsible citizens, religious people, our neighbors and even people participating in the Christian church."

J. C. Ryle (1816–1900), the first Anglican bishop of Liverpool, said something equally profound related to teeny-tiny sins. *"They may look small and insignificant, but mind what I say, resist them—make no compromise, let no sin lodge quietly and undisturbed in your heart."*

Be warned. Your clever, self-directed, and sinful side can justify anything. You play a dangerous game denying your conscience and convincing yourself that you are stronger than you really are. "Just because I smoked one cigarette doesn't mean I'm going to start smoking pot or doing cocaine." "Just because I didn't pay for a drink refill doesn't mean I'm going to be a bank robber." "Just because I sneak a peek at this website, it doesn't mean I'm going to spend hours searching porn sites."

When you start getting into arguments with yourself, you're guaranteed to lose.

How do we rescue ourselves from the slippery slope? The obvious answer is *don't take that first step*. After that you're going to need someone to speak truth into your life. Maybe it's an accountability partner, your entire small group, wise members of your church community, a caring parent, a loving spouse, or a courageous friend.

I hope and pray you have someone like that to snatch you at the top of that dangerous precipice. Ultimately, that slippery slope is not really their problem. It's yours. So do those wonderful people a favor. Don't put them on the spot. Don't make them work so hard or worry so much. Take it upon yourself to step back yourself from that alluring, yet treacherous cliff.[1]

29

Don't be **fooled** by the cult of
intellectualism.

*For it is with your heart
that you believe and are justified.*

ROMANS 10:10

It's quite fashionable these days to mock anyone who believes in a Creator God. From the news media to late night comics to any number of social commentators, there is an arrogant assumption that any intelligent thinker is certainly an atheist. God is mentioned on our money, but he's considered pretty much an antiquated superstition for chumps and suckers. Unfortunately, outside the walls of a church, very few people of influence have the courage to disagree.

Following that line of thinking, since there is no God, there is no universal or absolute truth. There is no right or wrong. Call it moral relativism. Or intellectualism. Students from kindergarten through grad school are told to pick any truth that suits their fancy.

I am on record saying that following God is an intellectual pursuit. We need to be thinking Christians, to be able to express reasons why we believe. That's includes logical and practical reasons. But also emotional and intangible reasons. Faith involves your brain and your heart.

Some people look at Creation and get both. Consider the universe, the Grand Canyon, or the biology of sight. Those things prove the existence of a designer. But they can also be emotionally overwhelming.

Digging through Scripture also satisfies both our intellect and our passions. The life of Jesus fulfills scores of Old Testament prophecies, which proves the trustworthiness of Scripture feeding our minds. The words of Jesus pierce our hearts.

The following story is a pretty good illustration of the difference between knowing something intellectually and believing it with all your heart.

A hundred years ago or so, a tightrope walker drew cheers from an appreciative crowd by confidently crossing over Niagara Falls on a rope. He asked the onlookers, "Now, do you believe I can push a wheelbarrow across and back?" They cheered even louder as he made that trip without hesitation. Then he asked, "Now, do you believe I can push this wheelbarrow across and back with someone riding inside?" They cheered wildly. He yelled over the roar, "Who will volunteer?" The crowd became very quiet.

The crowd believed the tightrope walker could do it. Intellectually, they were right with him. But they didn't have enough faith to trust him with their lives. The difference was that their heart could not accept what their brain had seen. They were living in conspicuous denial of obvious truth, spending their entire existence looking for reasons not to believe. Such is the desolation of modern-day intellectuals.

When I consider the empty life of intellectuals or militant atheists, it actually makes me a little sad. Their mockery of Christians proves their misery.

God—the ultimate life coach—knows and loves these men and women even as they deny his existence. When the Bible was first recorded, God knew that here in the twenty-first century so-called intellectuals would claim to be the gatekeepers of truth. That's why Colossians 2:8 includes this warning: "Don't let anyone capture you with empty philosophies and high-sounding nonsense that come from human thinking and from the spiritual powers of this world, rather than from Christ" (NLT).

If you find yourself walking down the path toward intellectualism or moral relativism, I invite you to pause. Don't be taken capture. Think *and* feel for yourself.

30

Don't make the **mistake**
of feeling **self-sufficient.**

If anyone thinks they are something
when they are not, they deceive themselves.

GALATIANS 6:3

It's possible that you've read this far and you are still on the fence about whether you need God's intervention in your life. You believe in God. You accept the fact that he is the Creator of the Universe. You even totally believe that he made you for a purpose. But somehow, you have taken the stance, Thanks God. But I can take it from here.

I'm a little embarrassed to say, "I can relate to what you're saying." Here's how that thought process might play itself out.

Thanks God for all you've done. Thanks for my ten fingers and ten toes. Thanks for giving me enough to eat and this beautiful place to live. Thanks for my wonderful spouse. Thank you for my job that helps provide food and security. Thanks for my good brain and the ability to think things through and get things done. I'll let you know if and when I need you again.

Is that totally absurd or what? That would be like Frankenstein's monster telling Dr. Frankenstein that he is now king of the castle. That would be like Apple thinking they are better off without the brilliant innovator and taskmaster, the late Steven Jobs. That would be like a four-year-old running away from home because he doesn't want to eat his broccoli.

In just about all cases you can think of, the Creator knows what's best for that which he has created.

You would think the human race would have learned that back in the Garden of Eden. Adam was living in paradise in fellowship with God. God gave him everything he needed including satisfying work and the perfect wife. God even made Adam and Eve in his own image. But that wasn't enough for the first couple. When they listened to the serpent and disobeyed God, they were saying pretty much the same as that italicized paragraph on the previous page. *Thanks for everything, God. But I'm smart enough to take it from here.*

Well, that's just delusional. In at least three different ways.

First, God is God and we're not. He knows how everything works. We can barely get our cappuccino maker to work properly.

Second, God does have our best interest in mind. He knows what's coming and has already prepared us to deal with every situation in the best possible way. Why not take full advantage of that?

Third, even if we knock it out of the park here in this world, there's still our ultimate future to consider. Yes, there are a handful of people who can turn their back on God and live pretty happily for 80 or 90 years. But that's a finger snap compared to eternity. I cannot recommend trading a few laughs here for a gazillion years gnashing your teeth in a ring of fire.

Still on the fence? Still thinking you can do life without God as your life coach? Good thing we're only halfway through. Keep reading.

31

I've got **good news** for anyone feeling **unworthy**.

For all have sinned and fall short of the glory of God.

ROMANS 3:23

As a life coach begins to identify obstacles to overcome, it often becomes clear that one of the obstacles is not really an obstacle at all.

What's holding you back is not a character flaw, a flurry of past mistakes, or lack of resources. There's no dragon blocking you from your destiny that needs to be slain. The doorway to your best life is open and accessible. All you have to do is walk through. But you cannot.

What happens is that an individual—like you or me—starts to think that we really don't deserve to do or be anything special. We think, *I'm not worthy.* This sense of inadequacy increases the more we begin to understand the character of God. His omnipotence, his omniscience, his omnipresence. His overflowing love. His righteousness. His glory.

Well, you know what? That line of thinking is not unreasonable. Compared to God, none of us deserve any claims in this life or the next. If you stop and think about it for even a moment, that should be quite clear.

You *are* unworthy. There is a name for the affliction. It's called sin. And it's a universal problem. All have fallen short of the glory of God.

Don't be dismayed. The day you realize your sinful condition may seem like the worst day of your life. But it's just the opposite. Consider the story of a fisherman named Peter.

Early in his ministry, Jesus strolled to the shoreline of the Sea of Galilee where a crowd gathers to hear him speak. At water's edge, he saw two boats left by fishermen after a disappointing day of work. Jesus got into Simon Peter's boat and asked to be taken just off shore so he could better address the crowd. When he finished speaking, Jesus told Simon Peter to go out and let down the nets for one more catch. Reluctantly, he did as he was told. The number of fish almost sank *both* boats. Simon Peter was aware of Jesus' reputation for miracle making. But at that moment, the fisherman knew without a doubt that he was not worthy of being in the presence of this miracle worker.

> When Simon Peter saw this, he fell at Jesus' knees and said, "Go away from me, Lord; I am a sinful man!" For he and all his companions were astonished at the catch of fish they had taken, and so were James and John, the sons of Zebedee, Simon's partners. Then Jesus said to Simon, "Don't be afraid; from now on you will fish for people." So they pulled their boats up on shore, left everything and followed him. (Luke 5:8 -11)

Only when Peter acknowledged his sinfulness—his unworthiness—was he capable of dropping his nets, leaving everything behind and following Jesus. Even for an impulsive fisherman, that's a startling decision. But it turned out to be a pretty good trade.

So, are you feeling unworthy? I hope so.

32

Sin **is** preventing you
from putting your past in the past
and living your **best life** today.

*Jesus replied, "Very truly I tell you,
everyone who sins is a slave to sin."*

JOHN 8:34

Until the last chapter, we haven't spent much time talking about sin. Back in chapter seven we looked at your list of desires and compared them to the seven deadly sins. But the point of that chapter was to get you setting worthy goals, not dealing with your sinful condition.

With God as your life coach, it's finally time. No more dancing around the issue. Let's face that problem head on. Let's admit that anyone feeling trapped, stuck in a rut, deeply frustrated, or not living up to their expectations can trace much of their personal bondage to sin.

Examples of sin that leads to enslavement are easy to come up with:

- Someone with a habit of lying will spend much of their time and energy lying to cover up the original lies. And worrying about getting caught.
- Sex outside of marriage opens the door to all kinds of diseases, unwanted pregnancies, and suspicions, worries, and intimacy issues with your spouse or future spouse.
- The selfish act of staring and poking at a smartphone screen while ignoring the people around you will isolate you from opportunities to love and be loved.
- Being envious of your neighbor's stuff leads to a life chasing things that inevitably leave you with a stack of credit card debt and an empty heart.
- If you dishonor your parents, holiday gatherings that should be filled with joy will instead foster bitterness and ill will. Or loneliness and heartache.

Sin robs the joy from life. You don't need the above list to prove that point. As your life coach, God continually points out areas of your life that are susceptible to sin. He uses emotions—remorse, sorrow, empathy—to identify sin. He uses your intellect and experience to reveal the negative repercussions of sin.

Even guilt and regret are valuable tools for identifying the sin in your life. Many life coaches might howl that guilt is a wasted or harmful emotion. Yes, it can be. But guilt is wonderfully valuable when you allow it to open your eyes regarding changes in your life that really should be made.

Each person is different, but sin is inevitable even for those who really do seek the voice and guidance of God.

If you think you've escaped the consequences of sin, you are mistaken. Some sins have immediate consequences and that can be a good thing. Witnessing the direct aftermath of sinful thoughts or actions may even lead you to pull the plug on that particular activity or habit.

Other sins have long-term consequences, and set you on that slippery slope described back in chapter 28. As a result, you may not identify your sin as sin until it is just about too late or has done quite a bit of damage to your health, relationships, and reputation.

In the end, the most vicious attribute of sin is that it separates us from God. If you have time, quickly turn to chapter 33.

33

Even worse,
sin blocks you
from spending
eternity with me.

But your iniquities have separated you from your God.

ISAIAH 59:2

Not sure about you, but I don't want to spend eternity in the place described in Revelation 21:8.

> But the cowardly, the unbelieving, the vile, the murderers, the sexually immoral, those who practice magic arts, the idolaters and all liars—they will be consigned to the fiery lake of burning sulfur.

That's where sin leads. Now, is there a literal fiery lake of burning sulfur waiting for all unbelievers? Maybe. Many people believe there is. But no matter what, it's pretty clear that eternal agony awaits a certain percentage of the population. Matthew 7:13 describes the two paths we can all choose. One is narrow; the other is the wide and well-traveled road leading to a drastically tragic resolution.

> You can enter God's Kingdom only through the narrow gate. The highway to hell is broad, and its gate is wide for the many who choose that way.

God desires all people to know and follow him, but he leaves the choice to us. As a result, way too many people are leaving earth unprepared and facing a future that is not kind. Most theologians suggest the worst part about hell is being separated from God.

But enough about hell. Let's talk about heaven. Is there really a crystal river (Revelation 22:1)? Are the streets really paved with gold (Revelation 21:21)? Is there an emerald rainbow arching over the throne of God (Revelation 4:3)?

Maybe. Many people believe so. But please don't worry about what you will be doing for all eternity. Despite the rumors, you won't be bored sitting on a cloud playing a harp or jealous that someone else has more crowns than you.

If you've had a fractured and frustrating life, you'll be especially blessed by the sweeping away of your old life. Revelation promises no more tears. "He will wipe every tear from their eyes. There will be no more death or mourning or crying or pain, for the old order of things has passed away" (Revelation 21:4).

But even those who have lived a comfy, carefree life will be blown away when they enter paradise. This is a place beyond our wildest imagination. "What no eye has seen, what no ear has heard, and what no human mind has conceived—the things God has prepared for those who love him" (1 Corinthians 2:9).

Finally, I recall my daughter asking, "Dad, will there be dogs in heaven?" I'll let theologians debate the finer hermeneutics and exegesis of the question. But here's my answer. "God will make sure you have everything you need to be overflowing with love, joy, peace, and contentment. If you need our golden retriever, Madison, to be there in order to be happy, she'll be there."

So how do we get invited to such a place? Well, it's really a matter of dealing with the one thing that is keeping you out. Once again, it's sin that separates us from God. Now and for all eternity.

34

The good news is that
I've provided an answer
to the problem of sin.
It's Jesus.

For Christ also suffered once for sins,
the righteous for the unrighteous, to bring you to God.
He was put to death in the body
but made alive in the Spirit.

1 PETER 3:18

I was a good kid. I almost never missed Sunday service. I rarely sassed my parents. With my best friend in fifth grade, I confess I did smoke cigarettes twice under the railroad bridge. A couple years later, I did sneak a peek at some naughty pictures that another friend brought to school. I had a little too much to drink a few times in college, but I certainly wasn't a party animal like some of my other fraternity brothers.

And that's one of the most dangerous deceptions there is: comparing ourselves to other humans. When the time comes, judgment is not a sliding scale. Compared to the neighbor down the street, you may be a saint, but you still fall short. Way short. The smallest sin makes us unworthy.

The entire narrative of the Bible confirms this truth, "The wages of sin is death" (Romans 6:23). As imperfect beings, we're cut off from God. We're facing spiritual, physical, and eternal death. We are guilty and someone has to take that rap. Without some kind of miraculous intervention, the blameworthy party—that's you and me—are going to be wading into that lake of burning sulfur.

The gospel has not yet reached every corner of the planet, but you certainly have heard the concept that Jesus paid the penalty for our sins on the cross. Did that truth sink in? Did it make sense? Can you even imagine the Son of God accepting the enormous weight and shame of every human sin—past, present, and future—and paying that ransom with his own life? It's almost impossible to wrap your brain around that truth, isn't it? A story might help.

It's 1941. A prisoner had escaped from the Auschwitz death camp in Poland. So the next morning, the Nazi guards assemble the entire camp and pick ten prisoners to die as a warning to the others. For every man who escaped, ten of his fellow prisoners would pay the ultimate price. One of the men chosen to die, Sergeant Franciszek Gajowniczek, has a wife and child, so without hesitation another prisoner, Maximilian Kolbe, steps forward saying, "Sir, let me take his place." The guards are stunned, even skeptical of Kolbe. But they allow this unheard of request.

Locked in a cell to starve to death, Kolbe spends his finals days comforting the other men with prayers, songs, and stories of Christ's sacrifice. After two weeks, six of the men have died. Of those who remain, only Kolbe is coherent, and he remains faithful to the end as those last four men are given a lethal injection of carbolic acid.[2]

Maximilian Kolbe, a Polish Franciscan Friar, becomes a twentieth-century example of what theologians call Jesus' substitutionary atonement for our sins. Like Jesus, Kolbe lived the words of John 15:13: "Greater love has no one than this: to lay down one's life for one's friends."

We can call Jesus the greatest teacher who ever lived. We can acknowledge that he modeled how to live and performed miracles. But his most significant victory and the reason God the Father sent him to become human was to die in our place. He is the sacrificial lamb. His blood washes clean the sinful condition of every believer.

35

What my Son did for you
is the **single greatest truth**
you need to know and accept.
But don't worry,
it won't **cost you anything**.

For it is by grace you have been saved, through faith—
and this not from yourselves; it is the gift of God—
not by works, so that no one can boast.

EPHESIANS 2:8-9

If someone rang my doorbell and attempted to hand me a giant cardboard check for a million dollars, I don't think I would take it. My skeptical nature would have me asking, What's the catch?

Few things are free anymore. There always seems to be an ulterior motive. An old friend buys lunch, then tries to get you to invest in his sketchy business venture. A teenager sets the table and cleans the bathroom without asking, only because a dismal report card is on its way. A seven-year-old becomes overly helpful and polite in early December.

But hold on. Some wise individual said, "The best things in life are free." And that's really an undeniable truth. Blue skies. A starry night. Cool breezes. Wildflowers. A mother's love. Hugs. Smiles. Faith. Hope. Love. A kind word from a stranger. These are all good things orchestrated from above. Delivered free, courtesy of your heavenly life coach.

Still nothing compares with grace, that wonderful free gift that transforms individuals from the inside out. Give God your heart, and he gives you a brand new one in return. "I will give you a new heart and put a new spirit in you; I will remove from you your heart of stone and give you a heart of flesh" (Ezekiel 36:26).

Allow me to repeat: grace is free. There's nothing you can do to earn it. You can't buy it. You can't trade for it. You can't hold it up and boast, "Look what I did." It's a love gift from the Savior. And once you've got it, there's nothing you can do to lose it.

So what does one do with such a wonderful gift? You tell others about it. You hang out with other believers so you can maximize the impact of the gift. You hunger to learn more about the gift giver. But most importantly, you become free to do your best work without fear.

Living under grace is like being one of the workers constructing the Golden Gate Bridge in the 1930s. As the story goes, dozens of men fell to their death during the early days of the project. After the installation of a safety net, not only were lives saved, but also productivity increased. Feeling more safe and secure, workers could concentrate on their job without fear of plunging into San Francisco Bay.

God loves you so much that once he gets a hold of you, he won't let you go. You are secure in your faith and wonderfully free to do great things and live your best life. You are free to risk it all for the glory for God. And, FYI, you are also free to sin. It's not recommended. You may feel a bit guilty. You'll want to confess and turn away from those new sins. But you're still human. God knows your heart. After all, he gave it to you. And his love will continue to hold you close and never fail you. That's true freedom in Christ.

36

So have you **accepted** the gift?
Are you sure?
It breaks my heart that so many people
stumble through life without
really knowing me,
hearing my voice, or savoring
my plan for their lives.

The man who says, "I know him," but does not do
what he commands is a liar, and the truth
is not in him. But if anyone obeys his word,
God's love is truly made complete in him.

1 JOHN 2:4-5

You might not think it was possible, but there are some people who are unsure whether or not they are Christians. Or more accurately, they may check a box or describe themselves as a "Christian," but they have not accepted Christ as their savior. As a result, they are missing out on the "abundant life" (John 10:10 KJV) and fail to experience "peace that transcends all understanding" (Philippians 4:7).

That's actually not surprising. There are probably millions of people who have been going to church for decades and really are not authentic believers. They may give financially to support a church. They may know the words to dozens of hymns. They're really nice to their neighbors, don't cheat on their spouse or their taxes, and even take in stray animals. But they haven't actually acknowledged the fact that they are sinners and broken in need of a savior, and they have not accepted grace. What's holding them back?

Let's dispel a few misconceptions.

- You have to do more than just believe that Jesus exists. Satan would be included in that category.
- You have to do more than just walk into a church building. Going to church doesn't make you a Christian anymore than walking into a garage makes you a car.
- You have to do more than just say a few magic words. Yes, there is a prayer of salvation. (We'll get to that in a few chapters.) But you have to say it

and believe it. "If you declare with your mouth, 'Jesus is Lord,' and believe in your heart that God raised him from the dead, you will be saved" (Romans 10:9).

- You have to make the decision for yourself. Neither your parents, your spouse, your mentor, nor your congressman can get you right with God. As a matter of fact, living in a Christian family or nation might even prevent you from seeing the sin and selfishness in your life.

- Don't assume your good deeds will outweigh your bad choices. We've already made the case that even one teeny-tiny sin separates us from God. Romans 3:10 confirms, "There is no one righteous, not even one."

Before you start thinking that following Christ is a list of things to do or not to do, let's reaffirm that grace is a gift. But the only proper response to such an incredible gift is surrendering your mind, heart, and will to God.

The late Charles Colson put it this way, "If Christ's lordship does not disrupt our lordship, then the reality of our conversion must be questioned."

With that in mind, are you questioning who is really lord of your life? The next three short chapters offer three more checkpoints to consider.

37

Check your guilt level.
Can you feel my heart breaking
or my righteous anger
each time you sin?

*If you are not disciplined—and everyone
undergoes discipline—then you are not legitimate,
not true sons and daughters at all.*

HEBREWS 12:8

Time for a little vital soul searching. In your conversations with your heavenly life coach, have you experienced some mixed feelings? He's making lots of sense, but he's also churning up some frustration? He's pointing out some areas of your life that you need to clean up and that's ticking you off a bit? Do those conflicting emotions include a bucket of excuses, insistence that your worst habit isn't that bad after all, a hunch that integrity is overrated, and a temptation to deposit this book in the trash?

Those are all human responses. And thoughts like that are totally understandable. But they also suggest that you haven't made a decisive decision for Christ and you really don't want to walk with God. *I couldn't possibly keep up with God's rules and expectations. I have my career, hobbies, and family obligations to work on right now. There's plenty of time to get right with God. And maybe he doesn't really exist anyway.* (Yikes, did you just think all that?)

Is this an accurate assessment? You're more than halfway through a book that ponders the idea that God would make a good life coach. But you're walking out of every session thinking, *I don't want to hear what he's saying.*

This human author has no authority to judge your relationship with God. But you *do* have that responsibility. Even if you're not looking forward to it, your goal should be to welcome God's discipline. When God's presence, Jesus' words, and the convicting presence of the Holy Spirit exposes your sin, that's a good thing. The Holy Trinity doesn't do that for just anybody. Only true believers.

When you get your faults out into the open, it's liberating. During the first years of our marriage—when I was a woefully unsuccessful office machine commission sales rep—my bride, Rita, would hide unpaid bills. Her goal was to spare me misery, but instead it made our financial matters worse. The day we laid all our bills on the kitchen table and began setting a budget prompted a difficult but welcome breath of fresh air. (And it led to a much-needed career change.)

In the same way, exposing and confessing sin robs Satan's power. He hates the light. Consider this thought from one of the last books of the Bible.

> God is light; in him there is no darkness at all. If we claim to have fellowship with him and yet walk in the darkness, we lie and do not live out the truth. (1 John 1:5-6)

Where are you walking? Are you living in the shadows, hesitant to come out into the light of truth? When God is lord of your life you will seek the light! When your sin is finally exposed and confessed, you will feel God's love deeper and stronger then ever. Yes, there may be repercussions. Hebrews 12:6 promises, "The Lord disciplines the one he loves." But that's good news. The best news ever.

38

Check your **hunger** for the Bible.
Does your heart
value the truth
of My Word?

---

*The law from your mouth is more precious to me
than thousands of pieces of silver and gold.*

PSALM 119:72

Over the past thirty years, I have produced thousands of radio broadcasts for ministries, volunteer organizations, and publishers. In many cases, we record more material than we need which requires me to listen and make time cuts to fit the length of the time slot. In the early days of my career, I had a strategy of which I am not proud. Imagine an author, speaker, or Bible teacher speaking for a minute or two on a topic such as parenting, evangelism, education, and so on. During the recording session, they may punctuate their message with a Bible verse or two. Well, if the broadcast was thirty or forty seconds too long, it was quite easy to simply cut the Scripture. The edits were typically effortless for the studio engineer. And the flow of the conversation never missed a beat. When the final broadcasts aired, the audience never knew. But they did miss the power of God's word. And that's a shame.

At the time—in the interest of meeting radio deadlines—I chose to literally discard God's Word on to the cutting room floor. Big mistake. God actually used that experience to convict me that we all need to learn to depend more on Scripture, not toss it away.

As the Bible itself teaches in Timothy 4:13, we need to read the Word in public. In 2 Timothy 2:15, we need to study and explain the Word. In Acts 17:11, we need to search the Scriptures to help us discern what is true. In Ephesians 6:17, we need to wield the Word like a sword. But most important of all—especially for any new believer— we need to hunger for God's Word. That spiritual appetite is described in 1 Peter 2:2-3: "Like newborn babies, crave pure spiritual milk, so that by it you may grow up in your salvation, now that you have tasted that the Lord is good."

Is that hunger in you? Have you tasted enough of Scripture that you appreciate its ability to transform your life?

A typical life coach might arm himself with pearls of worldly wisdom to inspire and motivate clients. But there's no real power there. God's words—which have been recorded faithfully in the books of the Bible—have great power.

How can words printed in a book have power? The first page of the gospel of John explains, "In the beginning was the Word, and the Word was with God, and the Word was God . . . The Word became flesh and made his dwelling among us" (John 1:1,14).

Jesus is the Word of God presented in human form. The Bible presents the love story of how and why God sent his Son to be the perfect teacher, perfect model, and perfect sacrifice for our sins.

Here's one last verse I pray you'll take to heart. Psalm 119:97, "Oh, how I love your law! I meditate on it all day long."

39

Check your willingness
to **suffer for Christ**.
At first, this idea may
not be easy to grasp.

Dear friends, don't be surprised at the fiery trials
you are going through, as if something strange
were happening to you. Instead, be very glad—
for these trials make you partners with Christ
in his suffering, so that you will have the wonderful joy
of seeing his glory when it is revealed to all the world.

1 PETER 4:12-13 NLT

This chapter may scare a few people off, and that would be a shame. But you can't deny the truth. Let's start with the promise of 2 Timothy 3:12: "Everyone who wants to live a godly life in Christ Jesus will be persecuted."

Even with God as your life coach, you may be thinking, *I didn't sign up for that. That must be one of those Scripture passages that relates to biblical times. I don't know anyone being persecuted these days.*

If that's what you're thinking, you would be wrong. The facts reveal that more people were persecuted and killed for being a Christian in the last century than all the other nineteen centuries before that.[3] Currently about 100 million Christians are being persecuted worldwide.[4]

These modern day stories are—at the same time—difficult to hear and inspiring. Churches burned. Believers driven from their homes. Pastors brutalized, jailed, and killed. In China, Sudan, Somalia, Malaysia, Pakistan, Bangladesh and dozens of other countries, governments prevent ownership of Bibles and sanction the harassment and even killing of Christians. Organization like Open Doors and The Voice of the Martyrs document thousands of cases per year, and come alongside these persecuted believers and their families.

You might assume that the church is crumbling in countries where such persecution is rampant. But the opposite is true, proving once again that God can turn evil into good, he uses these activities to build his church. As martyrs die, onlookers moved by their deep convictions are drawn to faith in Christ. In many cases, believers in these countries don't pray for the persecution to end, they pray for strength to be a witness to the lost. As Tertullian, an early church theologian, said, "The blood of the martyrs is the seed of the church."

Still, here in the west, most Christians should not expect to suffer persecution. Or should they? Maybe we should look for ways to invite persecution. Maybe we need to be asking ourselves, *What actions might I undertake that would give glory to God, but might result in my being persecuted for my beliefs?*

It might be standing up for a moral principle on the job. Quietly being the one employee who doesn't take home office supplies or pad their expense account. It could be challenging a friend to clean up his language and stop taking the Lord's name in vain. What if you actively began sharing the gospel with your new neighbor?

Would such actions lead to unbearable persecution? Probably not. But maybe it would get you out of your comfort zone. And that's a pretty good start.

40

Let's take care of **business**
right now.
Accept **grace**.

If you declare with your mouth, "Jesus is Lord,"
and believe in your heart that God raised him
from the dead, you will be saved.

ROMANS 10:9

Hopefully, you're feeling pretty good about your interaction with God as your life coach. You're becoming aware of his voice, love, and guidance. But, still there may be an entire level of relationship that you have not yet experienced. Grace opens that floodgate of never-ending communication, love, and confidence.

Ready to experience new purpose, the indwelling of the Holy Spirit, and eternal life? Of course you are. The only reason you might hesitate is because you're still feeling unworthy. We covered that back in chapter 31, but it's worth repeating: God, as your life coach, knows everything about you and still loves you. Romans 5:8 proves that point: "But God demonstrates his own love for us in this: While we were still sinners, Christ died for us."

So here's the plan. If you're not absolutely positive that you've accepted Jesus as your savior, you can take care of that right now. It doesn't cost anything. And you can do it without any intermediary—just you and God. All you really need is a clear head and a sincere heart.

Here goes. Read these words. Understand them. Accept them. And then declare them to God.

Dear God, I want to know you personally. But my sin keeps me at a distance from you, prevents me from my best life here on earth, and keeps me from spending eternity with you in heaven. I fully realize that someone has to pay the penalty for that sin and it should be me. But because you love me, you have provided a way out. You sent your son, Jesus, who never sinned,

to die on the cross and pay the penalty in my place.
That gift is free. All I have to do is truly desire to stop
sinning, believe in Jesus who died on the cross and
rose from the dead, and ask the Holy Spirit to guide
my life from now on. Lord, I choose right now to be-
come a child of God. Please come into my life. Amen.

If you prayed that prayer for the first time, then welcome into the family of God. If you haven't yet, you're
missing out on the greatest adventure there is. (And this
book will pretty much be a waste of time, so you can put
it down now.)

As a new believer, don't expect to feel all different—
although you might. But you can expect to experience
some new desires and insights. As we've said, you should
have a deeper curiosity for how the Bible applies to your
life. The meaning of difficult passages won't be instantly
clear, but your eyes will be opened. A bit of weight
should be lifted from your shoulders. Your sins have been
forgiven. Really. Psalm 103:12 says, "He has removed our
sins as far from us as the east is from the west" (NLT). At the
same time, moving forward, you'll be more keenly aware
of the times when you disappoint God. Don't worry, that's
a good thing.

God is now really your Father, Jesus is now your
brother, and the Holy Spirit is now your official guide.
Plus, because your name is now written in the book of life,
you and I can hang out in heaven. I'm looking forward
to it.

41

Congratulations,
you're a **new creation**.
Not only do you have a place
reserved in heaven, but you also
have access to a new resource.
A compass. A strategist.
A guiding light.

*Then, what looked like flames or tongues of fire
appeared and settled on each of them.
And everyone present was filled with the Holy Spirit.*

ACTS 2:3-4 NLT

Here's a thought. As a new believer, you really don't need to visit a life coach anymore. The moment you accepted that free gift of grace, you were blessed to receive the indwelling of the Holy Spirit, the ultimate life coach.

How does that work, you may be asking? Well, that's the same questions the apostles were asking at the Last Supper. Jesus was patiently explaining many vital precepts of the Christian faith to them including the earth-shaking events that would unfold over the following three days. Then he reveals that he would be leaving them, and going to the Father, but they won't really miss him because he will send "another Counselor."

Once it sinks in, the apostles' selfish thoughts are easy to imagine. *Another counselor? How could anyone or anything possibly replace Jesus, our living, breathing, walking friend and teacher?*

Jesus calmed their fears and eased their grief: "But very truly I tell you: It is for your good that I am going away. Unless I go away, the Advocate will not come to you; but if I go, I will send him to you. When he comes, he will prove the world to be in the wrong about sin and righteousness and judgment" (John 16:7-8).

Sure enough, the second chapter of Acts records the coming of the Holy Spirit at Pentecost, and Christians have been blessed by his supernatural guidance ever since. This new Counselor's purpose is to help us recognize right and wrong, to convict us when we fall short, and to empower us to act boldly in the face of injustice or evil.

I believe the Holy Spirit led Rosa Parks to hold her

seat on that Montgomery, Alabama, city bus in 1955. She knew she was breaking the law when she refused to give up her seat for a white passenger, but somehow she also knew she was doing the right thing. She later wrote, "I felt the presence of God on the bus and heard His quiet voice as I sat there waiting for the police." Mrs. Parks didn't set out to become a heroic symbol of the Civil Rights movement, but that's what happens when you allow yourself to be led by the Spirit.[5]

I believe the Holy Spirit also led Todd Beamer to help lead the charge up the aisle of a hijacked jetliner on September 11, 2001. When that plane nosedived into a Pennsylvania field, Beamer and his brave colleagues very likely saved the lives of hundreds of other Americans in some high profile building targeted for destruction. His courage and rallying cry of "Let's roll" still resonates in the grateful hearts of a nation that had quite a few heroes that day. No terrorist attack can ever claim victory when the Holy Spirit is at work.

Every authentic Christian is guided every moment of every day by the indwelling of the Holy Spirit. It's just that some of us choose not to follow his counsel. And it's also worth noting that the Holy Spirit is not some mystical phantom. He's a real person you can count on as an unending source of comfort, wisdom, intercession, and truth. Just as Jesus promised.

42

Now. **Finally.**
You are ready for the most
exciting adventure possible.
This is going to sound strange
coming from a life coach.
But . . . it's not about **you.**

Whoever finds their life will lose it,
and whoever loses their life for my sake will find it.

MATTHEW 10:39

Sorry. You very likely picked up this book because you wanted strategies for identifying, prioritizing, and fulfilling your own personal needs. News flash: Your best life isn't about you.

It was, a while back. When you were under three years old, life was about you and your needs. Spend any time with babies and toddlers, and you'll quickly discover their entire world is all about having someone else take care of them. Only later do small children learn life skills such as sharing, patience, and generosity.

Then, during the teenager years, many people go through another season believing the world revolves around them. They are taught that the secret to life is "being true to yourself," and the heck with everyone else. Those transitional years between childhood and adulthood are a catalyst for egocentric behavior. That shouldn't be surprising. Young people get their life coaching advice from teen magazines, social media, pop stars, and reality TV celebrities. Even school counselors, who are no longer allowed to take a moral stand but still try to guide young people through the tough decisions of life, are forced to encourage teen narcissism. Their advice? "Do what you think is right." "Follow your heart." "Only you can choose what is best for you." Without any moral foundation, that's a recipe for disaster.

When toddler adventures are all about the toddler, the result is a trashed playroom. That's not so bad. When teenage adventures are all about the teenager, the result is an unconstrained and shameless future. That's dangerous territory.

So what *should* your adventure be about? Do you want to live like a toddler or a self-centered teen? Not surprisingly, a better plan can be found in God's Word:

Do nothing out of selfish ambition or vain conceit. Rather, in humility value others above yourselves, not looking to your own interests but each of you to the interests of the others. In your relationships with one another, have the same mindset as Christ Jesus: Who, being in very nature God, did not consider equality with God something to be used to his own advantage; rather, he made himself nothing by taking the very nature of a servant, being made in human likeness. And being found in appearance as a man, he humbled himself by becoming obedient to death—even death on a cross! (Philippians 2:3-8)

Your most exciting and rewarding adventure requires you to look outside yourself. Your identity is not found in who you are, but in how God shows up in your daily life.

Billy Graham said, "Being a Christian is more than just an instantaneous conversion—it is a daily process whereby you grow to be more and more like Christ."

Think of it this way. We spend a lot of time trying to figure out *how to do* great things. Maybe we need to spend more time defining what the word *great* really means.

43

It's about me.

Bring all who claim me as their God,
for I have made them for my glory.

ISAIAH 43:7 NLT

The last thing you expect to hear from a life coach is, "Your life is about me." Typically, that's not a good sign.

But with God as your life coach, that's exactly what you signed up for. Because he's God, he knows you best. He also knows what's best for you. And, your best life is all about living to give him glory.

Maybe you've heard some version of that statement that before. "God made us to give him glory." Well, that can be a bit confusing. Especially because our human minds can't fully comprehend the definition or purpose of glory.

The Old Testament seemed to have a pretty good handle on the term. When God showed up in thunderstorms, plagues, cloud pillars, and fire from the sky, these were all examples of God's glory. Psalm 19:1 tells us, "The heavens declare the glory of God."

In the New Testament, God reveals his glory through the birth and life of Christ.

The Word became flesh and made his dwelling among us. We have seen his glory, the glory of the one and only Son, who came from the Father, full of grace and truth. (John 1:14)

Hebrews 1:3 confirms, "The Son is the radiance of God's glory."

The word "glory" actually appears more than 400 times in the Bible and scholars tells us it has a variety of meanings. For our purposes, let's just all agree that glory is larger than life and not something that can be held in your hand or easily described. It's like "beauty" or "love" or "serenity." It's difficult to put into words, but you know it when you experience it.

Because of our human limitations, glory might be the only way God can reveal himself to us. We would be overwhelmed if he showed up in person, so he sends his glory as a glimpse of his power and presence.

You might say glory is beyond human reach. Yet glory, only reachable through our relationship with God, Jesus, and the Holy Spirit, is our goal. Here on earth, we have no chance of understanding what glory is, but we can be sure that it's worth pursuing. Achieving glory is worth any sacrifice.

I consider that our present sufferings are not worth comparing with the glory that will be revealed in us. (Romans 8:18)

The action point from our heavenly life coach might be this: God doesn't need us to give him glory for some kind of ego boost. He *is* glory; he doesn't need *more* glory. He simply wants us to understand and acknowledge who he is and what he has done for us, so that we have a handle on how much he loves us. C. S. Lewis put it simply, "In commanding us to glorify Him, God is inviting us to enjoy Him."

Doesn't that make sense? We see his glory. We reflect

that glory back to him. Then we can rest in the comfort that our awesome God loves us and care for us.

It's not a once in a while thing. It's 24/7. Receiving and reflecting glory becomes our daily sustenance, "So whether you eat or drink or whatever you do, do it all for the glory of God" (1 Corinthians 10:31).

44

And it's about
others.

Jesus called the Twelve and said,
"Anyone who wants to be first must be the very last,
and the servant of all."

MARK 9:35

Serve others. That's not a difficult concept. But if you're still not 100 percent on board, you're in good company. The apostles needed to hear that message several times.

Walking from Galilee to Capernaum, Jesus had a one-sided conversation with his closest disciples. He described in detail how he would be betrayed and killed, and then rise from the dead. The apostles didn't understand what he was talking about, probably because they weren't really listening. They had been too busy arguing about which one of them was the greatest.

Jesus, of course, knew their every thought, but still he asked, "What were you arguing about on the road?" Mark 9 describes them as getting really quiet. Then Jesus straightened out their thinking: "Anyone who wants to be first must be the very last, and the servant of all."

On the Mount of Olives, Jesus presented a memorable parable on serving. He told the story of a king who promised his inheritance to those who fed the hungry, made room for a stranger, cared for the sick, or visited those in prison. Those humble servants were confused, "When did we do all those things?" The king replied, "Truly I tell you, whatever you did for one of the least of these brothers and sisters of mine, you did for me" (Matthew 25:40).

Perhaps, the grandest and most obvious lesson on serving delivered to the apostles was at the Last Supper. Jesus washed their dusty feet. And then told them, "I have set you an example that you should do as I have done for you" (John 13:15).

The apostles eventually got the message. Jesus the servant king made sure of that. Your heavenly life coach would also insist that any gifts, talents, and resources you uncover in the course of your sessions would be used best when used in service to others.

Serving others is how the last becomes first. Serving others is how you reinvest the king's inheritance. Serving others is how you follow Jesus' example.

The acclaimed preacher from the eighteenth century, John Wesley, expressed the same idea with this challenge:

"Do all the good you can,
By all the means you can,
In all the ways you can,
In all the places you can,
At all the times you can,
To all the people you can,
As long as ever you can."

The idea may sound impossible, even burdensome. But really, it's an attitude adjustment that will make all the difference—in your life and in the lives of everyone you meet. "In humility value others above yourselves, not looking to your own interests but each of you to the interests of the others" (Philippians 2:3-4).

45

Not sure, where to **start**?
Allow me to help you
set your **priorities**.

Set your minds on things that are above,
not on things that are on earth.

COLOSSIANS 3:2 ESV

Let's all agree that the way to get your priorities right is to set your mind on heaven. Unfortunately, that's not always easy. You're here. You're not dead yet. There are things that need to get done. Diapers to change. Bills to pay. Schedules to keep. Bosses, teachers, and spouses to keep happy. Work to do.

There's a great old adage that I'd like to use to illustrate this point. "When you're up to your neck in alligators, it's difficult to remember that your original objective was to drain the swamp."

In other words, your objective from God as your life coach can be clearly defined: *to get to heaven and take as many people with you as possible.* But you can easily be distracted when you find yourself overwhelmed with responsibilities and deadlines here on earth. What's more, you're kind of hoping that your time in heaven doesn't start for a few years or more.

Here's another old saying that might add to this conversation. "Don't be so heavenly minded that you're no earthly good."

We all know people who walk through life with a permanent look of optimism plastered on their face even as the world crumbles around them. In a very real sense, they have their spiritual act together. I'm a little jealous of those people. They are being "heavenly minded," while many of us are "earthly-minded." The Bible suggests that those are really the only two choices that exist.

There are many whose conduct shows they are really enemies of the cross of Christ. They are headed for destruction. Their god is their appetite, they brag about shameful things, and they think only about this life here on earth. But we are citizens of heaven, where the Lord Jesus Christ lives. And we are eagerly waiting for him to return as our Savior. (Philippians 3:18-20 NLT)

To be more heavenly minded, it may help to think of ourselves as citizens of heaven and just visitors here on earth. That may be the greatest truth delivered by any life coach ever. That understanding—that we are on the threshold of heaven—will help us plow through inevitable losses, disappointments, frustrations, and moments of discouragement.

When you're feeling physically unattractive, you need to be able to look in the mirror and think, *You know, what? That's really not a big deal. This imperfect body will be glorified after my time on earth is done.* (Philippians 3:21)

When your best friend or worst enemy buys a big house in a nice neighborhood, your citizenship allows you to think, *Good for them! My entire family has a mansion waiting in heaven.* (John 14:2)

When you miss out on a promotion or lose the championship game, there's no need to be jealous. Just think, *I'm looking forward to a crown of righteousness, which is a much bigger honor.* (2 Timothy 4:8)

As you consider the best location for your permanent home address, allow me to toss out another quote from C. S. Lewis, taken from his book *Mere Christianity*: "Aim at heaven and you will get earth thrown in; aim at earth and you will get neither."

46

You've got some **work** to do.
But that's **good news**.

But be doers of the word, and not hearers only,
deceiving yourselves.

JAMES 1:22 ESV

Are you plowing through this book because you want to do great things? That's fantastic. With that in mind, your heavenly coach has a very specific assignment that will have you taking great strides toward that goal. Close this book, pick up your Bible, and read the entire book of James. Really. It's only five chapters and will take about ten minutes.

Before you go, consider this. James emphasizes the importance and value of work more than any other book of the Bible. Some scholars have even suggested that it conflicts uncomfortably with the rest of Scripture. By emphasizing the connection between belief and action, they say it is promoting justification by works. Let me assure you, grace is a free gift and always will be. But thanks to James—and the Holy Spirit—we should continually feel inspired to demonstrate our faith through our works. Consider these passages:

> Do not merely listen to the word, and so deceive yourselves. Do what it says. (1:22)

> Faith by itself, if it is not accompanied by action, is dead. (2:17)

> Who is wise and understanding among you? Let them show it by their good life, by deeds done in the humility that comes from wisdom. (3:13)

If anyone, then, knows the good they ought to do and doesn't do it, it is sin for them. (4:17)

On the topic of doing great things, here's a life-changing and surprising tip on what that means for you. *Do stuff that comes easy.* If you can dance, dance. If you can write, write. If you can build, build. If you can hug, hug.

Does that sound obvious? Too many people miss that point. They think that work should be work—tedious, unfulfilling, and backbreaking. As if God wants us to be miserable. Why is that? Maybe their father came home from work every day muttering how much he hates his job, and they thought that was how life worked. Maybe they're trying to prove how courageous and disciplined they are by sticking to a job they hate. Maybe they think that if something is easy, it's not worth doing. Maybe no one ever challenged them to follow their dreams.

So here is your challenge. Do not be one of those people who perpetually sets aside activities you enjoy, hoping to get to those things on a free weekend or in retirement. Consider the possibility that what you enjoy—your natural giftedness—should be your career. Or perhaps a full-time ministry.

To put it another way, don't exhaust yourself trying to be good at something you don't care about. Instead, take something you're already good at, and put that same effort into being great!

Your life coach would agree. God doesn't want you to settle for less than your best. You don't have to be a CEO of a Fortune 500 company. You don't have to see your face on the cover of *Forbes, Inc.,* or *Entrepreneur.* But you do have to polish your skills in your sweet spot. Proverbs 22:29 says, "Do you see someone skilled in their work? They will serve before kings."

One final aside: Don't quit your unfulfilling job based on this short chapter. There are aspects of every job that are no fun. There are seasons of life that will require you to sacrifice and put your dreams on hold. But do keep checking in with your life coach.

47

Let's go back and **review** your plan.
It's really not a bad plan.
But it's **limited** by the world.

The mind governed by the flesh is death,
but the mind governed by the Spirit is life and peace.

ROMANS 8:6

Let me guess your plan. Through middle school, enjoy a nice mix of school, hobbies, and goofing around. Get serious about a few things in high school. But not too serious. And maybe your first kiss.

Jump into college, the military, or the working world and find some success. Make some intelligent, fun friends. Make enough money to have your own place and take a vacation once in a while. Become good at your job. Gain respect and stretch yourself a bit.

Find the right person and fall in love. Get married. Have a kid or two or three. Gain more authority, respect, and financial security. Leave the workforce while you're still young enough to enjoy retirement. Die peacefully surrounded by family and friends.

Sound good? Any life coach—conveniently located in this world—would call that a pretty good plan. For the 78.7 years (on average) that you live on this earth, you could do a lot worse. One recommendation is to take the above plan and just do it. Then we could end this book right here. Except for one thing. Somewhere, somehow, you got a little off track from that plan of yours. You had a few setbacks—some you caused yourself and some were out of your control. Or maybe there has been a total derailment.

Everyone is different, and I'm not going to list all the possible circumstances that caused you to swerve or crash. But you need to know that very few people—maybe zero percent—chug along through life without getting sidetracked from their pretty good plan.

The goal is to get you back on track to finish your plan, right?

Hold on. If you've been paying attention at all, you know that your goal is not to complete *your* plan, but to discover and complete *God's* plan for your life and beyond. Previous chapters have offered quite a few hints about listening to God as your life coach. That includes assessing your resources, removing obstacles, accepting grace, and putting others first. But there may be an even easier way to confirm that your plan is heading the right direction.

In Acts 17, there's a delightful story of Paul and Silas spending three days in the city of Thessalonica teaching about Jesus. The two men were feeling especially empowered because they had just escaped prison in Philippi with the help of an earthquake, and actually led the jailer and his family to believe in God in the process. The best part of the story is the words the ticked off Jewish leaders used to describe Paul and Silas in their official complaint to the Thessalonica city council. They said, these men were causing trouble and had "turned the world upside down" (Acts 17:6 NKJV).

So there's your hint. Look at what the world is doing. *And do the opposite.* By turning the world's values upside down you will be walking with your feet firmly planted among the stars. You'll be standing on an unshakeable foundation established by God. Maybe even walking on sunshine.

Colossians 3:1 puts it this way: "Since you have been raised to new life with Christ, set your sights on the realities of heaven" (NLT).

Applying the reality of upside-down living means attitudes like hate, greed, racism, and wickedness are exchanged for love, generosity, fellowship, and righteousness. Make sense?

48

Take **your** good plan.
And let's **compare** it
to **my plan**.

So you should earnestly desire the most helpful gifts.
But now let me show you a way of life that is best of all.

1 CORINTHIANS 12:31 NLT

This may be the chapter you have been waiting for. You need to know that God, as your life coach, has a specific strategy for every area of your life and is "setting it apart" for his glory. How does that sound?

If you like the idea of being "set apart," then you are officially onboard for "holiness."

What, you say? *I didn't sign up to be holy.* Well, yes you did. The Hebrew word for holy is "qodesh" and that translates as "set apart." Several verses of Scripture confirm the idea that those who believe in Christ are "holy."

For it is written: "Be holy, because I am holy." (1 Peter 1:16)

You must be holy because I, the LORD, am holy. I have set you apart from all other people to be my very own. (Leviticus 20:26 NLT)

Make every effort to live in peace with everyone and to be holy; without holiness no one will see the Lord. (Hebrews 12:14)

A lot folks might bristle at the word "holy." That's not surprising. If being holy is your goal, then all sorts of expectations or burdens might be heaped on top of you. Someone striving for holiness may be asked to leave their comfort zone once in a while. Holy people do things like volunteer in soup kitchens and travel to far-off places to be nice to people who don't look like us. That's a bit scary.

Being holy also means we're calling ourselves *exceptional*. And that just sounds like one big ego circus. Plus, most of us just want to fit in. No one wants to be labeled as radical, special, or peculiar. Those are the kids who got bullied back in middle school.

Here's the problem: "holy" is a label that has lost its original meaning. It sounds preachy or sanctimonious. Well, maybe it's time to reclaim the idea of being holy. The rest of this book is going to help you recognize the glory and rewards of holiness. How—on your own—you might possibly do good things. But if you allow God to work through you—you will achieve great things.

That idea is described well in Ephesians 3:20: "Now all glory to God, who is able, through his mighty power at work within us, to accomplish infinitely more than we might ask or think" (NLT).

The final chapters of this life coaching devotional are dedicated to helping you take your gifts, experiences, and relationships . . . and set them apart. Claiming them as holy. Accomplishing more than we can imagine.

You already have so much to offer. Your heart, mind, and soul are burning with a desire to give back to God. Your plan is solid, but in God's hands it can deliver so much more.

Keep reading. We're going to take your *good plan* and help you see how with a little effort—or by taking a gutsy leap of faith—you can align it with *God's plan*.

49

In your good plan,
your character and integrity
emerge from a personal code of ethics
guided by cultural norms.
In my plan, you are
made in my image.

Do not conform to the pattern of this world,
but be transformed by the renewing of your mind.
Then you will be able to test and approve what
God's will is—his good, pleasing and perfect will.

ROMANS 12:2

Do you like what you see going on in the world? It's such a beautiful place. There exists kindness, forgiveness, and gentleness. There's music, art, literature, and so much more that lifts our spirits and confirms that life is indeed worth living. Fitting into this amazing world would certainly be part of your good plan, and might even be the driving force influencing your perspective on right and wrong.

But there are also plenty of things going on—brought on by humanity—that are not so pretty. Racism. Cults. Addictions. Prostitution. Child abuse. Anorexia. Sexually transmitted diseases. Bulimia. Slavery. Suicide. Date rape. Adultery. Shoplifting. Alcohol abuse. Sexting. Abortion. Murder. Hate crimes. Gender confusion. Pornography. Drunk driving. Terrorism. Human trafficking.

Want to hear more? I didn't think so. Frankly, it's not pleasant even to type that list, much less dwell on it and consider the brokenness of our world. But the point should be obvious. We cannot allow who we are to be shaped by a culture that is saturated with so much evil. We need to identify another foundation or force to help shape our morality, character, integrity, decisions, outlook, and behavior.

Consider this Bible passage describing the first moment that humans existed. "So God created mankind in his own image, in the image of God he created them; male and female he created them. God blessed them and said to them, 'Be fruitful and increase in number; fill the earth and subdue it'" (Genesis 1:27-28).

Have you considered the idea that you were made in

the image of God? And what does that mean? Well, we're not talking about a visual likeness. When I look in the mirror, I am quite certain God doesn't look like me. As you've been spending time with God as your life coach, you never pictured him looking like you, have you?

In general, theologians agree that "being made in God's image" means that we were created as God's representatives on the earth. To be fruitful, multiply, and care for the planet, the living kingdom, and each other. Sometimes, we haven't done a very good job. Nonetheless, because of our intrinsic human dignity as image-bearers, God put us in charge.

So—as God's representatives—how should we respond?

Being loving caretakers for all of creation should be driving our moral code. We may even be able to take that list of disgusting human activities on the pervious page, and base our values on the exact opposite. (Building an upside-down world as discussed in chapter 47.) That leads to ideas like respect, love, chastity, placing high value on life, honoring God's design, and obeying God's laws.

Also, being made in God's image, we should strive to embody his attributes. God is just, so we should be just. God is truth, so we should seek truth. God is love, righteousness, faithfulness, and so on.

Can you see how your good plan—depending on the moral code of the world—falls far short of God's will for our lives? Let's continue in our quest to move from our good plan to God's perfect plan.

50

In your good plan,
your **financial security**
grows out of your hard work
and wise investments.
In my plan, everything
you have belongs to me.

"Bring the whole tithe into the storehouse,
that there may be food in my house. Test me in this,"
says the Lord Almighty, "and see if I will not throw open
the floodgates of heaven and pour out so much blessing
that there will not be room enough to store it."

MALACHI 3:10

If you're like most people, your income, budget, and cash flow are not exactly where you want them to be. Still, you are committed to the idea that hard work, a modest lifestyle, cutting coupons, saving for a rainy day, and saving for retirement are solid financial concepts. You even toss a few bucks in the basket on Sunday and feel pretty good about that. Does that sound like your well-thought-out financial plan?

Let's see what your heavenly life coach has to say on the topic. The Bible has some 500 verses concerning faith and about 500 on prayer. But there are more than 2,300 on money and possessions. Many of those passages do encourage hard work and wise stewardship. Others warn about swindlers, sluggards, and the distractions of wealth. Some passages encourage prudent saving, while others are quick to remind us not to "store up treasures here on earth, where moths eat them and rust destroys them, and where thieves break in and steal" (Matthew 6:19 NLT).

Another recognizable verse on money is Matthew 6:24, "No one can serve two masters, for either he will hate the one and love the other, or he will be devoted to the one and despise the other. You cannot serve both God and Money" (ESV). That verse suggests a sense of urgency. We can't serve both. We need to choose.

Another biblical concept we can't avoid is tithing, giving ten percent of your income to the Lord's work. It's an Old Testament concept.

Be sure to set aside a tenth of all that your fields produce each year. (Deuteronomy 14:22)

Men were appointed to be in charge of the storerooms for the contributions, firstfruits and tithes. (Nehemiah 12:44)

The concept of tithing is reaffirmed in the New Testament (see Luke 18:12; Matthew 23:23; Hebrews 7:8). Interestingly, later references to tithing confirm how important it is. . . but also suggest that ten percent may not be enough.

With all that being said, here's the breakthrough idea. Ready? *It's all God's anyway.* Psalm 24:1 confirms, "The earth is the LORD's, and everything in it, the world, and all who live in it." We should actually be grateful he let's us keep ninety percent. Besides, God doesn't need our money. He wants our hearts. And he doesn't want things like greed, accumulating more stuff, or taking care of a bunch of temporary possessions to distract us from his love and purpose for our lives.

Said another way, our life coach knows the best way to escape the clutches of money is to give some of it away. It's freeing. It's rewarding. It's refreshing. God promises, "A generous person will prosper; whoever refreshes others will be refreshed" (Proverbs 11:25).

51

In your good plan, your work and **career** provide income and the satisfaction of accomplishment. In my plan, you're **working for me**.

Whatever you do, work at it with all your heart, as working for the Lord, not for human masters.

COLOSSIANS 3:23

One of my favorite conversation starters is to ask people about their career path, starting with their very first paycheck. I'd love to hear yours. But for now, this one-sided conversation will usher you swiftly from my first job to where God—as my life coach—has planted me today.

During my school years, my jobs included newspaper delivery, busboy, bagger, waiter, carpenter, cotton-candy maker, boxcar unloader, and department store Santa Claus.

My first full-time jobs after college were selling photocopiers for the A.B. Dick Company and law books for Matthew Bender & Company. Both jobs were brutal. God rescued me from commission sales and I became a novice copywriter for a boutique ad agency on Chicago's famed Michigan Avenue where we helped Frito Lay name and position a new salty snack which would become "SunChips." After less than a year, I moved to a bigger agency with accounts like Midway Airlines, Kroger, and Corona Beer.

My growing faith and desire for a shorter commute eventually led me to a small agency and recording studio in the suburbs that served Christian ministries and publishers.

My next job was not a job at all. For more than 20 years, I have been a freelance writer, producer, author, creativity trainer, speaker, and consultant. Dozens of clients have come and gone. And on those occasions when I thought I couldn't pay the bills, God would provide. Really.

Looking back, I realize that my good plan was not a plan at all. I just kept working hard and doing the best I could at the next opportunity. (Which I guess is a sort of a plan.) But I also clearly see God's hand in every one of those jobs and job changes. And that's the realization I hope you also experience.

Give your best effort and expect God to walk beside you on your career path. Every workplace will yield opportunities for you to grow or to help someone else grow. Every boss and colleague has value in the eyes of God. Every position can't be your favorite job ever or your fantasy career. But there's a reason you're there, and you may not even know that reason for a decade or more. Or ever.

In a way, your career path parallels the process of evangelism. When someone comes to faith in Christ, it probably wasn't as a result of one person delivering one perfect biblical precept. It was more likely a series of individuals coming alongside that person planting seeds with moments of love, correction, listening, questioning, challenging, and modeling. Eventually one of those seeds germinates and the seeker turns toward the light and says, "Grace please." Those seed planters won't all know each other. And the seed planting may be years apart. Or it could all happen in a flurry. But the point is, it all works together. And that's how heaven gains a new permanent resident.

Likewise, your assignment in any field, calling, or occupation is the same. Bloom where you're planted. And replanted. And expect it all to work for glory of God.

So remember: do your work for God and God will work in you. And don't forget, wherever you punch your time clock, look for your own God-given opportunities to plant some seeds—or water or pull weeds or harvest—for the gospel.

52

In your good plan,
marriage fulfills our need for
lifelong companionship and romance.
In my plan, marriage is all that *plus*
it reflects the **relationship**
of Christ and the church.

Husbands, love your wives,
just as Christ loved the church
and gave himself up for her.

EPHESIANS 5:25

A re you married? If you're not, please don't skip this short chapter. Yes, it's about marriage, but it's also about something much, much bigger.

Let's first agree that marriage is not a business relationship, legal contract, or a stage of life that happens for convenience or by accident. The second chapter in the Bible describes it quite emphatically: "A man leaves his father and mother and is united to his wife, and they become one flesh" (Genesis 2:24).

What does it mean to "become one flesh"? I think it happens when a couple says "I do" on their wedding day. It also happens in the marriage bed—emotionally, spiritually, and physically. Becoming one flesh also describes the journey of a husband and wife traveling through life together. They carry each other in good times and not-so-good times. They celebrate and console. They love each other unconditionally. They give and receive.

Ephesians 5 sheds light on the marriage relationship, beginning in verse 21, "Submit to one another out of reverence for Christ." That's pretty clear. Each and every believer is expected to have the heart of a servant and put first the needs of others.

There's some controversy surrounding the next couple verses. "Wives, submit yourselves to your own husbands as you do to the Lord. For the husband is the head of the wife as Christ is the head of the church, his body, of which he is the Savior" (Ephesians 5:22-23). But really, the controversy disappears as soon as you read those two verses in context. The previous verse (5:21) calls for mutual submission. And the next several verses deliver an explanation for the depth of sacrifice that men need to have for their brides. Specifically, Ephesian 5:25 says, "Husbands, love your wives, just as Christ loved the church and gave himself up for her."

Men and women have different needs, and these passages are unmistakable. Husbands need to lead. Wives need to feel cherished. To drive that point home, husbands are given a role model for the courageous and sacrificial love they need to have for their wives. Men need to love their wives *as Christ loved the church*. Wow. That is a monumental, unfathomable amount of love.

Speaking to guys for a moment, you need to be on board with this challenge. Loving your wife sacrificially means putting her well-being before your own when it comes to your time, energy, resources, creativity, and even your will. That's right. You lead . . . for her sake. If she's unhappy, suffering, discouraged, ignored, or feeling unloved, there's a problem. Your mandate is to do what it takes to rescue her, just as Jesus gave his all for us.

As for those called to singleness, you are also challenged to submit to others with a servant's heart. And you can rest in the assurance that Christ's love washes over every member of his church.

53

In your good plan,
a family offers each
member security, provision,
and a personal board of advisors.
In my plan, family is all that *plus*
the building block of society.

Honor your father and your mother,
so that you may live long in the land
the LORD your God is giving you.

EXODUS 20:12

You gotta love the idea of family. Family is where kids learn to love and be loved. Family is where kids first learn to smile, talk, count, read, catch a ball, and bake cupcakes. Moms and dads tuck kids in bed, check homework, and set curfews. Kids listen, learn, and sometimes push boundaries. Belonging to a family is all part of God's best design. Yes, families come with conflicts and misunderstandings. But they work. And that's why your good plan includes family.

Jesus—even though he was fully God—needed to be part of family. He was born to a real-life human mom and dad. Luke 2:52 records how twelve-year-old Jesus sought out some enlightenment from teachers in the temple courts, but he returned home to his family so that he could grow "in wisdom and stature, and in favor with God and man."

The Bible endorses families by including quite a few admonitions for parents and kids. The emotional, spiritual, and physical well being of individuals, communities, and churches depends on healthy families.

Fathers, do not embitter your children, or they will become discouraged. (Colossians 3:21)

Urge the younger women to love their husbands and children . . . so that no one will malign the word of God. (Titus 2:4,5)

Listen, my son, to your father's instruction and do not forsake your mother's teaching. (Proverbs 1:8)

(A church leader) must manage his own family well, having children who respect and obey him. For if a man cannot manage his own household, how can he take care of God's church? (1 Timothy 3:4–5 NLT)

Family matters on so many levels. Your heavenly life coach even dedicated one of the Ten Commandments to esteeming and preserving the family.

While all the commandments come with an assignment (put God first, speak truth, don't kill, and so on) only one also includes a promise. Number five promises that honoring your parents establishes long life in a stable location granted by God Himself. At the first presentation of those stone tablets, the Israelites were receiving a promise that extended into future generations. God was promising the Promised Land.

Today, our application of the fifth commandment also extends far beyond our family. When we heed the fifth commandment—to honor your father and mother—we are acknowledging that families will always have a place and be a priority in the eyes of God.

Finally, the idea that intact, nurturing families are the building blocks of communities, nations, and the world was clearly established in one of the first directives given by God to Adam and Eve in the Garden of Eden. Referring to the first man and woman, we're told, "God blessed them and said to them, "Be fruitful and increase in number; fill the earth and subdue it" (Genesis 1:28).

54

In your good plan,
your **friends** and acquaintances
expand your worldview and provide
new perspectives on life.
In my plan, relationships build
the **kingdom** of God
here on earth.

As iron sharpens iron, so one person sharpens another.

PROVERBS 27:17

How might you define a friend? Let's check in with Pinterest.

- "Someone who loves you when you forget to love yourself."
- "Someone who knows your weaknesses but reminds you of your strengths."
- "Someone who sees the first tear, catches the second, and stops the third."
- "Someone understands what you're not saying."
- "Someone who makes the good times better and the hard times easier."

How does a friend be a friend? Let's check Scripture.

Therefore, as God's chosen people, holy and dearly loved, clothe yourselves with compassion, kindness, humility, gentleness and patience. Bear with each other and forgive one another if any of you has a grievance against someone. Forgive as the Lord forgave you. And over all these virtues put on love, which binds them all together in perfect unity. Let the peace of Christ rule in your hearts, since as members of one body you were called to peace. And be thankful. Let the message of Christ dwell among you richly as you teach and admonish one another with all wisdom through psalms, hymns, and songs from the Spirit, singing to God with gratitude in your hearts. And whatever you do, whether in word or deed, do it all in the name of the Lord Jesus, giving thanks to God the Father through him. (Colossian 3:12-17)

That's quite a bit to chew on. First, understand that these verses are talking about people living as followers of Christ. If this includes you, then you should expect to claim your role as a victorious heir to the kingdom of God, but also expect to humble yourself as a servant to others in gratitude for what God has done for you.

Digging in, the above New Testament passage on "how to be a friend in Christ" opens with five character qualities that display quiet strength. Next we read the formula for forgiveness, which is all wrapped up with love, the peace of Christ, and an attitude of gratefulness. Then the passage gets even more serious, presenting a challenge to anyone who cares about others—including friends, acquaintances, even strangers you may never meet. We are to live the gospel joyously, so that it's attractive and compelling. We should bask in the truth and richness of God's Word. Singing, speaking, and acting with one purpose. That is, to tell others about Jesus.

God as your life coach might choose to say it more simply, "Iron sharpens iron." When followers of Christ hang out, everyone wins. As a believer, your attitude and actions should make just about everyone you meet keenly aware that you have what they need.

Are you on Pinterest? How about sharing this pin on your board? "A true friend is someone with the courage to tell you about Jesus."

55

In your good plan,
health and physical fitness
help you play hard and live long.
In my plan, it's time
to put your body to work.

For physical training is of some value,
but godliness has value for all things,
holding promise for both the present life
and the life to come.

I TIMOTHY 4:8

A few chapters ago you read that your finances are not your own. All your bank accounts and worldly possessions belong to God. How did you respond to that idea? Did you dash off a big fat check and send it with an apology note to your pastor because you haven't been faithfully tithing a full 10 percent on every dollar you've earned since high school? I hope not. (Unless you were miraculously moved to such an extreme response.)

Well get ready for this idea from 1 Corinthians: "Do you not know that your bodies are temples of the Holy Spirit, who is in you, whom you have received from God? You are not your own; you were bought at a price. Therefore honor God with your bodies" (6:19–20).

In other words, your body, health, stamina, longevity, and well being also belong to God. How does that idea hit you? Well, it's actually true for *two* reasons. He made you. And his Son paid the ultimate price for you.

While you mull that over, consider this thought. You've heard that your body is a temple. You shouldn't smoke or drink. You should exercise thirty minutes a day, get eight hours of sleep, and eat your veggies. Blah-blah-blah. That's not a new concept.

If you've been hanging around a church for any length of time, you may have heard and dismissed this idea as overkill. In many ways, identifying your body as a temple feels like just another burden of guilt for anyone who is not in peak physical shape. Romans 12:1 seems to add to the burden with the expectation "to offer your bodies as a living sacrifice, holy and pleasing to God."

But what does all this really mean? Honestly, it's not a burden at all. It means *every* part of your physical self is an instrument designed to be used by God. That includes specific body parts like your smile, voice, vision, ears, feet, hands, arms, brains, and brawn. Suddenly, we've moved from a toilsome theory to real-life application.

All of us can and should smile for God. And use our voice to speak out in love for who he is and what he's done. On God's behalf, we should look around our neighborhoods to see what needs to be done or who needs someone just to listen. Are you walking, healing, and hugging for Jesus? Since God owns your mind, what problems can you solve for him? Since God owns your shoulders and strong back, what job does he have waiting for you?

A well-know quotation, sometimes attributed to Teresa of Ávila, the sixteenth-century writer and church reformer, says it well:

> "Christ has no body now but yours. No hands, no feet on earth but yours. Yours are the eyes through which he looks compassion on this world. Yours are the feet with which he walks to do good. Yours are the hands through which he blesses all the world. Yours are the hands, yours are the feet, yours are the eyes, you are his body. Christ has no body now on earth but yours."

As your life coach, God is most certainly saying to you, "I don't care how much you bench press or how fast you run 26.2 miles. But I do care how you use your body to serve me."

56

In your good plan,
education leads to knowledge,
respect, and influence.
In my plan, those attributes
equip you to point others to me.

Always be prepared to give an answer
to everyone who asks you to give the reason
for the hope that you have.
But do this with gentleness and respect.

I PETER 3:15

If you spend any time on a secular college campus you will be exposed to a big fat dose of deconstructionism and moral relativism. These philosophies are among the current atheistic ideologies that suggest there is no such thing as truth and there is no right or wrong. Professors seem to love Friedrich Nietzsche, the nineteenth-century philosopher who famously said, "God is dead," and who also wrote, "You have your way, I have my way. As for the right way, it does not exist."

Because these professors are paid real money to think deep thoughts, they must be right, right? Well, not necessarily. Let's consider their motivations. Most self-proclaimed deep thinkers found on college campuses—as well as coffee shops and hipster hangouts—really just like the sound of their own voice. They're not delivering big ideas. They're arrogantly endorsing a small, selfish way of looking at the world.

Nietzsche is declaring, *There is no god. There is no moral compass. It's all about me and what I want.* Such a thought process is more than selfish—it's dangerous—for several reasons. If I do what I want and you do want you want, what happens when we disagree? Which one of us gets our way?

Worse than that, what if both of our desires are nasty, ugly, and evil? Nietzsche said the right way "does not exist." Under that ideology, one king has full authority to call for the elimination of blondes while the neighboring king can choose to eliminate redheads. A declaration of war will soon follow. That may sound silly, but, hey, Nietzsche's world has no rules.

Anticipating this kind of nasty, ugly, evil thinking, the Bible warns, "Don't let anyone capture you with empty philosophies and high-sounding nonsense that come from human thinking and from the spiritual powers of this world, rather than from Christ." (Colossians 2:8 NLT)

The plan for doing battle with "empty philosophies and high-sounding nonsense" is to become a thinking Christian. Not following blindly. Not counting on the faith of your parents for your salvation. Not walking into a church once in a while. But working through doubts and diligently pursuing truth. Jeremiah 29:13 offers this challenging reminder: "You will seek me and find me when you seek me with all of your heart."

God as your life coach would endorse the idea of seeking knowledge. That includes formal classroom education, apprenticeships with experienced craftsmen, reading well-written influential books (including those written by existentialist philosophers like Nietzsche and Kierkegaard), archaeological digs, counting the stars, safaris, expeditions, sabbaticals, mentoring, seminary, Bible reading, and Bible studies. And listening intently to anyone over ninety years old.

God is truth. So the more you know, the closer you are to truth and the closer you are to God. The goal is not to know enough to win a screaming match with an agnostic know-it-all. The goal is to have your own hope based on the gospel. And let your light shine so that people ask you about the source of that hope. And then respond—brilliantly and engagingly—with respect.

When it comes to drawing others to the good news of the gospel, someone once said, "It pays to be winsome. In order that you may *win some* for Christ."

57

In your good plan,
your **creativity** generates
something that has
never before existed.
In my plan, your creativity
proves I exist.

So God created mankind in his own image,
in the image of God he created them.

GENESIS 1:27

O f all the creatures on the earth—because we are made in God's image—only humans can create.

Animals don't create. Many species may exhibit amazing abilities and unique skills. Beavers build elaborate dams. Oysters create pearls. Dogs, dolphins, and other animals communicate within their species and with humans. Bees and wasps build intricate nests utilizing a structural design of distinct hexagonal chambers. But let's be clear. These activities are either innate or learned over time and generations. The fact that some animals appear to be creative is simply more proof that the Creator was wonderfully inventive as he was mapping out the ecosystem of our world.

Human creativity is reflected throughout Scripture. Adam was charged with naming the animals. Israel got creative and designed a coat of many colors for his youngest son, Joseph. In Exodus 31:3-5, an Israelite named Bezalel is described as filled by God "with all kinds of skills—to make artistic designs for work in gold, silver and bronze, to cut and set stones, to work in wood, and to engage in all kinds of crafts." David played the lyre; that's why the shepherd boy was first summoned to King Saul. The architecture of Solomon's Temple revealed stunning creativity. And, the last thing Jesus and the apostles did together at the Last Supper was sing a hymn.

Please don't insist you're one of those people with zero creativity. Your life coach would be sad to hear you say that. After all, his assignment for you may be to help reclaim the arts from the today's blight of so-called "entertainment" that's often violent, depressing, graphic, filthy, angry, and devoid of hope. And it's not just edgy or extreme artists. Mainstream books, movies, art and music regularly assault our senses.

In some ways, we shouldn't be surprised. Film producers, songwriters, artists, publishers, and network executives are just doing their job. Their assignment is to make as much money as possible for their companies. If they don't believe in God, why would they feel compelled to follow a biblical worldview when pushing their products to the marketplace?

The best way to respond to art that drags down humanity is to create art that uplifts. For centuries the most brilliant musicians, artists, and writers lived with one purpose and passion—to honor God. You know these masterpieces. *The Sistine Chapel. The Last Supper.* Handel's *Messiah.* "Jesu, Joy of Man's Desire," *The Pilgrim's Progress. The Lord of the Rings.*

I understand you don't think of yourself as a da Vinci, Handel, Michelangelo, Bach, Bunyan, or Tolkien. But you'll never know how your work will impact others until you step out in faith. The art form doesn't matter. From dance to weaving to calligraphy. It could be anything.

Where do you start? By following the clear instructions of Philippians 4:8: "Finally, brothers and sisters, whatever is true, whatever is noble, whatever is right, whatever is pure, whatever is lovely, whatever is admirable—if anything is excellent or praiseworthy—think about such things."

Think on such things. And then follow your creative instincts. Your noble, lovely, admirable artistic expression will surely point others to God. Just as he intended.

58

In **your** good plan,
your **faithfulness** brings comfort
and direction in this life.
In **my** plan, my faithfulness delivers
power from the next life
to make a **difference** in this life.

I am the vine; you are the branches.
Whoever abides in me and I in him,
he it is that bears much fruit,
for apart from me you can do nothing.

JOHN 15:5 ESV

Somewhere along the way we humans got things mixed up. Especially those of us who live in first world countries. Somehow, we decided that we generate our own power. We have all the answers. We can do all things all by ourselves. We don't need anyone else.

That idea has even trickled into the psyche of those who identify themselves as Christians. We have the unfortunate impression that *our* faithfulness to God is what brings purpose to our lives and punches our ticket to an eternity in paradise.

That's backwards thinking. That's putting you and me in charge, and that would be a mistake. I know I would mess things up. And I am pretty sure you would, also. For sure, you have spent quantity and quality time with God as your life coach. That's a good thing. But you should know by now that we need him, not the other way around.

Yes, we can and must have faith in God. And yes, we have much to do. We can deliver hope. We can spread joy. We can seek knowledge. We can feed the hungry. We eagerly quote Philippians 4:13 to the world: "I can do everything through Christ, who gives me strength" (NLT). But we forget that unplugged from Christ we are powerless.

Anything we achieve is totally dependent on God. He is the true vine. That vine includes the roots and full access to soil, water, and sun. We are mere branches. Cut us off and we are fruitless. Our strength comes only from the faithfulness of our heavenly Father, our life coach, the Alpha and Omega. And it will never end, "Your faithfulness continues through all generations; you established the earth, and it endures" (Psalm 119:90).

Good news. God's enduring faith even runs deeper than you can imagine. There will be times when we attempt to cut ourselves off from the vine. By accident or quite intentionally. It may go back to our pretense that we are totally self-sufficient. Or it may be those times when we allow some silver-tongued serpent to convince us we would be better off without the rules and confinement of being in God's garden. We let down our guard. We conform to the world. And we lose our faith. But we don't lose God's faith.

Remember who God is. God is truth. God is love. God is righteousness. God is faithfulness. He is unchanging. 2 Timothy 2:13 promises, "If we are unfaithful, (God) remains faithful, for he cannot deny who he is" (NLT).

There's something very attractive about that truth. Just as God's love makes us more loving. Just as God's peace brings us peace. God's unwavering faithfulness should make us want to be more faithful.

That's not just a good plan. That's God's plan.

59

Can you see how
my plan and your plan
are the **same plan**?

*Now we see things imperfectly, like puzzling reflections
in a mirror, but then we will see everything
with perfect clarity. All that I know now is partial
and incomplete, but then I will know everything completely,
just as God now knows me completely.*

I CORINTHIANS 13:12 NLT

I'm not a car guy. I'm also not a go-with-the-crowd guy. So back in the 1980s, when every young family was getting a minivan, I wanted no part of it. Our paid-for hatchback that got almost 30 miles to the gallon was doing just fine.

Well, Rita eventually talked me into test-driving one. And it was an instant blessing, especially when it came to wrestling with infant car seats and kids' sports gear. We would own four of those brilliantly designed vehicles over the next twenty years.

I admit I was wrong. My plan was okay. But my wife's plan was so much better. Now, I wouldn't dare suggest that following God's plan is like buying a minivan, but the analogy hopefully works.

My eyes were opened at that test drive. And owning that first minivan was a life changer. (By the way, I totally understand that minivans are a joke now. But for at least two decades—especially with five kids—they ruled.)

Here's the point. I urge you to develop a plan. Do your due diligence. Research. Ponder deep thoughts. Dream big dreams. But stay open to God's guidance. Listen for his voice. And when you least expect it, you will gain an unbelievable clarity of vision.

That's when you will see that your good plan is primed to morph into a magnificent plan designed exclusively for you by the Creator of the universe. As the above verse promises, your knowledge of everything that matters will be complete, reflecting the way God knows you completely.

The ability to align your plan with God's plan is astonishing to consider. But here's something that's even more astonishing. When you embrace God's plan, the joy and completeness you will feel has nothing to do with your immediate surroundings or circumstance. Again. The joy and completeness you will feel has nothing to do with your place or position in this world.

You will not have to travel to the Himalayas or the Galapagos Islands to experience God's glory in your life. You don't have to spend forty years in a desert, build a temple, or follow a star. You don't have to be famous, wealthy, or even healthy to secure the peace that surpasses all understanding.

Finding God. Being set apart for God. Pointing others to God. Having relationships with others who love God. That's not just good stuff, it's great stuff. Actually, it's God stuff.

At this point, you may be thinking, *If I don't get cash, fame, or physical healing, why bother? What's in it for me?* The obvious answer is eternal life, which is more than enough to make your decision to follow Christ worthwhile. Plus, there's the gift of the Holy Spirit and a sense of purpose in life beyond yourself. Perhaps most surprising is something that's simply not available to those who don't know Christ. That's contentment.

> I have learned to be content whatever the circumstances. I know what it is to be in need, and I know what it is to have plenty. I have learned

the secret of being content in any and every situation, whether well fed or hungry, whether living in plenty or in want. (Philippians 4:11-12)

Contentment is not for sale. You can't fake it. It's not a natural state found in our finite world. It's a gift. With that gift, everything you need to see, you will see with perfect clarity. There are no more puzzling and confusing reflections in a hazy mirror.

Indeed, we're not home yet. On this side of eternity, you may still have questions. But that's okay. Because you know there are answers to those questions that are more satisfying than you could ever imagine yourself. That's all part of the plan.

60

Let's circle back
to where we started.
I haven't changed.
Have you?

The Lord directs the steps of the godly.
He delights in every detail of their lives.

PSALM 37:23 NLT

We've covered a lot of ground. In fifty-nine life coaching sessions, we asked some tough questions, explored your hopes and dreams, identified your gifts and resources, and overcame some obstacles. With courage, you admitted your brokenness and may have even found new life in Christ. In the last ten chapters, you began to see that your good plan was actually a launching pad to help propel you to God's plan for your life.

Which just leaves one question. Are you having fun yet?

Is that startling to consider? Is fun not your typical topic for a life coach? Had you come to the conclusion that following God was some kind of burdensome list of rules to follow and grueling tasks that led to no earthly reward? Then you haven't been paying attention. (Or maybe, this author wasn't quite clear enough.)

Back in chapter 49, we said the purpose of life for a follower of Christ is (1) to get into heaven and (2) take as many people with you as possible. Let's add a third purpose—and this is serious business—have fun along the way.

That third objective is intricately linked to the first two. If you're heaven bound, then you can experience uninterrupted joy because you know that any pain, frustrations, or discomfort here on earth is temporary. Also, by sharing God's love with others, there's going to be a deep joy in your life rooted in making a meaningful impact.

Does that make sense? Have you faithfully been considering God's life coaching advice and still find yourself yearning for joy? One of the final thoughts shared by Jesus at the Last Supper may bring clarification. He said, "Until now you have not asked for anything in my name. Ask and you will receive, and your joy will be complete" (John 16:24).

So ask. For anything. If you ask God for anything—in the name of Jesus—your prayers will be answered and joy will follow. What does that joy look like? How will it manifest itself in your life?

Every person is different, of course. You may give and get more hugs. You may sleep sounder with sweeter dreams. You may more fully appreciate hummingbirds, daisies, rainstorms, puppies, and fireflies. You may suddenly become nicer to store clerks and restaurant servers. Perhaps, you will become more aware of things unseen like angels, heaven, and the heartfelt invisible emotions of people who pass through your life. You may witness joy showing up in unlikely places—such as prison cells, cancer wards, pregnancy crisis centers, bumper-to-bumper expressway traffic, AA meetings, funerals, and at the foot of the cross. There's a very good chance that family gatherings will feature less judgment and more laughter and memory-making.

If you'll allow me another quote from C. S. Lewis, "Joy is the serious business of Heaven."

So that would be the pot of gold at the end of this rainbow. The colorful arc of this book—sixty life coaching sessions with God—should lead you to a place that's both familiar and jaw-dropping. This is your life. Not just scrubbed clean, but all new.

A life of meaning.

A life of wonder.

A life of joy.

Notes

1. A portion of this chapter is excerpted from *10 Conversations Kids Need to Have with Their Dads*, Jay Payleitner, Harvest House, Page 159.

2. https://www.amazon.com/Year-Life-Verse-Devotional-Book/dp /1414312628/ref=sr_1_12?s=books&ie=UTF8&qid=1473803195&sr =1-12, page 119

3. http://www.christianity.com/church/church-history/timeline/1901-2000 /modern-persecution-11630665.html

4. http://www.reuters.com/article/us-religion-christianity-persecution -idUSBRE9070TB20130108

5. https://www.amazon.com/Under-God-TobyMac-ebook/dp/0764200089 /ref=sr_1_1?s=books&ie=UTF8&qid=1474083528&sr=1-1&keywords =under+god+dc+talks Page 234

About the Author

Prior to becoming a full-time author and speaker, **Jay Payleitner** served as freelance radio producer for a wide range of international movements including the Salvation Army, Prison Fellowship, Bible League, Voice of the Martyrs, Josh McDowell Ministry, and National Center for Fathering.

As a family advocate, life pundit, and humorist, Jay has sold more than half-million books including *52 Things Kids Need from a Dad*, *The Dad Manifesto*, *Lifeology*, and *What If God Wrote Your Bucket List?* His books have been translated into French, German, Spanish, Slovenian, and Russian.

Jay is a national speaker for conferences, retreats, and weekend services with messages on parenting, marriage, creativity, storytelling, and finding your life purpose. He has been a guest multiple times on *The Harvest Show*, *100 Huntley Street*, and *Focus on the Family*. Jay also served as Executive Director of the Illinois Fatherhood Initiative.

Jay and his high school sweetheart, Rita, live in the Chicago area where they raised five great kids, loved on ten foster babies, and are cherishing grandparenthood. There's much more at JayPayleitner.com.

IF YOU ENJOYED THIS BOOK, WILL YOU CONSIDER SHARING THE MESSAGE WITH OTHERS?

Mention the book in a blog post or through Facebook, Twitter, Pinterest, or upload a picture through Instagram.

Recommend this book to those in your small group, book club, workplace, and classes.

Head over to facebook.com/worthypublishing, "LIKE" the page, and post a comment as to what you enjoyed the most.

Tweet "I recommend reading #IfGodWereYourLifeCoach by @JayPayleitner // @worthypub"

Pick up a copy for someone you know who would be challenged and encouraged by this message.

Write a book review online.

Invite Jay to speak at a retreat, outreach, or weekend service on the topic, "If God Were Your Life Coach."

Visit us at worthypublishing.com

 twitter.com/worthypub

 worthypub.tumblr.com

 facebook.com/worthypublishing

 pinterest.com/worthypub

 instagram.com/worthypub

 youtube.com/worthypublishing